The
Change
Cycle

The Change Cycle

How People Can Survive and Thrive in Organizational Change

Ann Salerno & Lillie Brock

BK

Berrett–Koehler Publishers, Inc.
San Francisco
a BK Business book

Berrett-Koehler Publishers, Inc.
235 Montgomery Street, Suite 650
San Francisco, CA 94104-2916
Tel: (415) 288-0260 Fax: (415) 362-2512   www.bkconnection.com

Ordering Information

Quantity sales. Special discounts are available on quantity purchases by corporations, associations, and others. For details, contact the "Special Sales Department" at the Berrett-Koehler address above.

Individual sales. Berrett-Koehler publications are available through most bookstores. They can also be ordered directly from Berrett-Koehler: Tel: (800) 929-2929; Fax: (802) 864-7626; www.bkconnection.com

Orders for college textbook/course adoption use. Please contact Berrett-Koehler: Tel: (800) 929-2929; Fax: (802) 864-7626.

Orders by U.S. trade bookstores and wholesalers. Please contact Ingram Publisher Services, Tel: (800) 509-4887; Fax: (800) 838-1149; E-mail: customer.service@ingram publisherservices.com; or visit www.ingrampublisherservices.com/Ordering for details about electronic ordering.

Berrett-Koehler and the BK logo are registered trademarks of Berrett-Koehler Publishers, Inc.

Printed in the United States of America

Book Producer: Publication Services, Inc.   Production Manager: Susan Yates
Book Designer: Dorothy Evans   Copyeditor: Carol McGillivray

Berrett-Koehler books are printed on long-lasting acid-free paper. When it is available, we choose paper that has been manufactured by environmentally responsible processes. These may include using trees grown in sustainable forests, incorporating recycled paper, minimizing chlorine in bleaching, or recycling the energy produced at the paper mill.

Library of Congress Cataloging-in-Publication Data
Salerno, Ann, 1957-
    The change cycle : how people can survive and thrive in organizational change / Ann Salerno & Lillie Brock.
        p. cm.
    ISBN 978-1-57675-498-6 (pbk. : alk. paper)
        1. Organizational change. 2. Change (Psychology) 3. Social integration. 4. Self-realization. 5. Satisfaction. I. Brock, Lillie, 1956- II. Title.

HD58.8.S2533 2008
650.1—dc22   2008008534

First Edition
13   12   11   10   09   08   10   9   8   7   6   5   4   3   2   1

Dedicated to

Bradford F. Spencer, Ph.D.

Mentor and Friend

Contents

Preface

Herding frogs. The image, you might say, "jumped" out at us as we thought about ways to visualize what it can feel like when you're in the middle of a difficult change at work or in the nature of your professional life. Weathering change can be chaotic, frustrating, even maddening. At its worst, a challenging or sudden change can do such a number on your confidence that you might experience moments verging on hopelessness—and we thought trying to herd a bunch of frogs might have the same effect if you stayed at it long enough (say, anything longer than a minute).

Helping you move successfully through your change is the reason we wrote this book. Our goal is for your experience not to feel like frog herding. On a muddy riverbank. With a hundred bullfrogs. And in truth we set our sights higher than that: our hope is that there are lessons in this book that can help you not only survive your change but *thrive* in it. What's more, you will be better equipped for the next work change to come your way. And the six-stage model we discuss can guide you through changes outside work as well, so whatever you find of value this time around will be there for any significant future change in your professional or personal life.

This book helps you navigate your way through change by utilizing The Change Cycle model (see front inside cover). The model depicts the six predictable and sequential stages of change and the specific thoughts, feelings, and behaviors associated with each stage. Each chapter covers one of the six stages of The Change Cycle and features stories of workplace change, draws on recent organizational and psychological research, and highlights the most important things we have learned in fifteen years of studying and teaching change. Here and there you might run into a little humor, too. Change at work is hard enough— we didn't want this book to stare back at you like a dour academic. Or a displeased boss.

The Change Cycle has been road tested by people in companies and organizations across America and on four continents. It has been used by people contemplating a career change, by the self-employed, by the recently promoted, and by the recently laid off. The model works for people up and down an organization and that is how we wrote the book: it is meant for anyone who works, manages, supervises, or leads.

At times our advice is addressed specifically to employees. In other places the insights are directed toward managers. That said, we believe there's value for everyone in these moments because they bring you inside the perspective of those on another level of your organization. Plus, any targeted discussion is set against the background of what we *all* experience going through change.

There are shelves of books about organizational change. This book is about what it actually feels like during a work change, and how to come out the other side. *The Change Cycle meets people where their emotions are,* said a friend of ours who read the book in draft form. We think that's about right. We hope that as you read on, this book does indeed meet you where your emotions are. And in so doing, that it helps you gain insight into your change experience—insight that will help move you through the process.

Jump in.

Ann Salerno and Lillie Brock

Change@Work

Note from Ann
"Conversations at 37,000 Feet"

I travel a lot. Often my seat neighbors will ask me what I do. "I'm a corporate trainer," I say. "I help organizations trying to change. Because no matter what their business, how well they manage change will determine their success. They need to be ready."

Change in the same sentence as *success* often gets their attention, and then they ask, "How do you train a company to change?"

My answer is always the same: "Well, once I teach a company's people the stages of change and how to navigate them, workplace changes are much easier to take."

Marketplace shifts, new industry standards, a current event with company impact—businesses are hit with myriad changes. I make the point that when speaking of change, the emphasis must go to the company's *people.* Change only becomes a reality within a business or organization when its individual members commit and carry out the new initiative, accommodate the new structure, follow the new system, or turn out the new product.

This sometimes causes a moment of skepticism in my seatmates. "Yeah," they say, "that's all we ever hear—change this, change that." They comment on how fast change happens, how it happens all the time—how important change is—but no one ever seems to know how to do it well, whether personally or professionally.

At this point in my airplane conversation, I usually admit that despite fifteen years as a "change agent," I, too, struggle with life's changes at times—at home and at work. Some changes are great—a new love, a promotion, a financial bonus—but many changes in life (maybe most) are simply hard, really hard: a company layoff, a divorce, the death of a loved one, a business failure. They hurt. They make us feel out of control.

Knowing that even a change professional can have trouble coping with change seems to somehow comfort my seatmates. The next question they typically ask is, "Can you help regular people deal with change?" By this time I know a conversation about some difficulty of theirs is coming. So I make it easy for them by explaining that managing change is more about understanding and accepting a set of common human reactions than it is about some kind of "attitude adjustment."

Change is life, life is change. It just happens, like the weather. Changes result from chance, choice, or crisis, and are generally unpredictable. But the process of "how" we move through life's changes is predictable, I explain. This usually brings a measure of both curiosity and relief.

In my work I have seen many employees struggling to adjust and regain their productivity following some new initiative or shift in leadership and direction. Both professionally and in my personal life, I have seen people grasping at straws trying to make sense of circumstances that leave them at a loss as to what to think or do next.

I've seen people in "change pain"—sad, mad, angry, blaming, afraid—their sense of loss and confusion often driving their lives into uncharted emotional waters. These are places they wouldn't have to go (or at least enter so deeply) if they understood more about the universal process of change: what to do, and what not to do, as they progress through the regular and sequential pattern of experiences that is The Change Cycle.

By this point in the conversation I'm drawing on a napkin, explaining how we as humans are wired to react and respond to change in six stages, how these stages are defined by characteristic thoughts, feelings, and behaviors, and how (best yet) they occur in an order that can be anticipated, so much of the mystery of *What's happening?* or *What will happen next?* is eased.

Then I ask my seat neighbor if there is a change in their life that is causing some angst. Sensing I won't judge them and seeming appreciative to have a chance to talk, they tell me things like, "My husband just got laid off," or, "My mother recently passed away." "My oldest just dropped out of college," they might say, or, "My best friend has breast cancer." Sometimes it's just, "I have a new boss." I listen as they tell their stories. The way they talk—the words they choose, the thoughts and emotions they describe—are clues I need to determine which stage they are in now. I show them where they are, explain what it means, and suggest what they might consider or explore or do next. Sooner or later, I assure them, they'll feel back in control, though they may not ever actually like or appreciate the change.

I love this moment. It's the one when they get it—"it" being the reminder that whatever they are going through, it's only temporary. After all, I tell them, just because you have a flat tire doesn't mean you have forgotten how to drive.

And then we share a laugh.

Knowing what's likely to happen next is the part that gives people the most comfort. Yes, when brought to their attention, they see the pattern—the natural sequence of change, just like there is a cycle of the seasons or phases of the moon.

Through the years, I've heard hundreds of change stories. At 37,000 feet I have listened to tales of life's battles lost, and life's wars won, of changes that brought some people to their knees and propelled others to new emotional heights. For all the good and bad that can be said about life, the fact is we will all face challenging transitions—personally and professionally—that will continue at varying intensities throughout our lives.

Learning to manage change is a skill we all need to acquire, improve, and master—in all aspects of our lives. I hope this book will assist you in improving your change resiliency and help you find your footing during times when the going gets tough.

The Focus of Our Book Change@Work

When we speak of work or professional changes, we mean both the "big ones" and the mundane ones, the ones that took weeks or even months to complete and the ones that kicked in overnight, the ones that seemed ridiculous but turned out pretty good, and the ones that appeared to be no-brainers but crashed and burned. This book provides a framework to assist you in gaining perspective on the change and its impact, insight that will guide you through the transition.

Our central goal is to help you take responsibility for how you react and respond to a changing work environment by giving you tools of self-awareness and assessment—instruments to light the curves and bumps on your change road. It's all about getting through the change emotion and commotion with minimal damage to your blood pressure, career, relationships, productivity, and confidence—whatever your role in the company or organization.

It is our belief that there is no magic way to achieve a pain-free experience of a significant work change—or a significant life change, for that matter. But understanding the regular, cyclical nature of the process helps you navigate the change in a conscious, anticipatory way, minimizing the fear, loss, resentment, and anxiety which to one degree or another accompany so many changes in work and life.

For all we know about the science and predictability of change, there is still the mystery of intensity when it comes to individual reactions. A change that might rock one person's world can be a speed bump to another. Each of us experiences change with our own scoreboard correlating to where we are on our path through life. And this variability extends to companies—collections of individuals—as well. It is amazing to be in one workplace where productivity might decline simply due to the distraction of a new food-service vendor, while at another company such a decline would only result from layoffs or similar major change.

In the pages ahead, you will encounter many different examples of workplace change. Some we might call "change bombs"—devastating losses to companies and individuals: a plant closing, a product recall, workplace violence, executive corruption. Other changes might seem trivial in comparison, but as we suggest above, almost any company change can have real impact, and depending on certain factors (management style, workplace culture, change track-record), it can seriously affect morale—to the point where what would appear to be a "small" change can give rise to employee anger, blame, resistance, and lethargy.

In a way, organizational change brings a set of dynamics akin to family or relationship dynamics: little things can become big things over time; employees have "long memories." If management is cavalier in making changes that impact employee convenience (parking, food, dress code), when it comes time for a company to initiate a major change, reaction will be partly predicated on employees' prickly memories of what has come before. The bottom line? The price of frequent, chaotic, or mismanaged change can be high. Change management requires care; no change is too small for skilled handling.

We wrote this book for anyone charged with communicating, carrying out, integrating, or simply dealing with a challenging work transition. We focus on the *human* perspective. We take as seriously as we can everything that comes into play during a change at work, not only company rollout strategies and management-employee relations but also the effects on people's work perform-ance, schedules, interactions with colleagues, energy lev-els, morale, and life at home.

A change at work is like throwing a rock into a lake—there will be ripples, and often they extend into your non-work life too. We try to never lose sight of the fact that the separation between work and home can be narrow, often very narrow. Happily, in helping you better deal with workplace change, these pages teach lessons that carry over into your nonwork life—a positive not only for you and those close to you, but also for your company or organization. Fewer ripples at home mean fewer at work—and of course the reverse is also true.

The Challenge of Change

Why is organizational change so difficult?

Because teams, departments, sites, mom-and-pop entrepreneurial businesses, companies small and large, school systems, governments, and global organizations cannot effectively transform unless their workers and members are committed to the change. This holds true whatever the impetus, crisis, challenge, or well-constructed strategic plan, whatever the rewards of success or consequences of failure. People must buy in.

No matter the value or process employed to make the change, there will be unforeseen implementation issues and underlying dynamics created by the workplace environment and the organization's communication style. If change is initiated in a decree from the top brass and the news then makes its way down through the ranks, what we call the "they factor"—*How did* they *decide?*, "*How do* they *know?*, They *have no idea*—can arise among employees and lodge a stick in the spokes of the transition.

Another challenge stems from the gap in change-assimilating between those company leaders who conceived of the change and those who one day learn about it. Execs and upper management can be significantly further along in The Change Cycle than those at the employee and lower-management levels who are suddenly mandated with "making it happen."

When change is initiated within the workforce itself, it has a different set of implementation issues. By and large, these issues work themselves out more quickly, and the change impacts service and product quality standards for the good. Communication is more relevant and timely. There's more ownership of the need to change, which leads to superior identifying of problems and solution-creating, a circumstance less prone to the-old-way versus the-new-way struggle some top-down decisions create.

Supervisors and managers are the most important link to the potential success of any change, because it is up to them to carry the ball for the ongoing communication after the initial announcement. Successful strategic initiatives and organizational change require above-average attention and commitment to communication, above-average leadership and management skills. Executives, managers, and supervisors must be willing to go beyond job and industry know-how to valuing learning and excelling at people skills—aka communication skills—in order to successfully facilitate and manage the ongoing changes at all levels within any organization. This includes being willing and able to look forward with fervor to what might be.

The first and most significant issue is this: managers and leaders must be willing and able to manage themselves. Individually, they must take responsibility for how they tend to react in changing environments. In dealing with change, managers and leaders must address their own thoughts, feelings, and behaviors before they can address anyone else's.

Often workplace higher-ups say things like, "We have to beat this thing." Or, "Change or die." Or, "We gotta swim with the sharks." These types of comments are indicative of the survival mentality common in the early stages of change. "Can you swim with the sharks?" should not be the focus or concern. "Can you swim at all?" is the issue. If yes, teach others. If no, grab your floatie and jump into the water—we can change that.

The Pull of the Past

One of the reasons people find change so hard is they have never been taught to understand the emotional and cognitive challenges that change creates. The latest brain science and cognitive psychology studies continue to point to *memory* as a key indicator of how we will react during an unfolding change situation. Whether you are reading this book as a worker, manager, or leader, you probably don't need research to persuade you that unresolved thoughts and feelings about "how some things were handled" in previous company changes are a significant reason employees can have a hard time believing or trusting their employer when a new change is introduced. Our recollections of unfortunate or difficult past changes can insinuate themselves into our general outlook and cause skepticism, cynicism, bitterness, and other states not conducive to workplace concentration and performance.

Memories have a dramatic impact on how we interpret what is or might be happening to us and why. And even if the memories aren't actually resourceful—meaning there is no close connection between the past change and the one you are experiencing now—the brain has a way of editing, reshaping, and generalizing the "historical" information, calling it useful and sending it to you anyway. You then try to superimpose it on the current situation as if this could be the key to solving your issues or problems. The good news is, it could be valid and helpful information that gives you direction. The bad news is, it could turn out to be a distortion or generalization that takes you down the wrong dark alley.

The Role of "Schema"

Human beings have always had a complicated relationship with change. Is it good? Is it bad? The combination of our memories and the power of our personalities (whether we motivate ourselves with new challenges or a need for security) is what pushes or pulls the change to the good or bad side of the line. Just why is our memory so powerful a driver of our thoughts, feelings, and behaviors? Because as humans, we first view change—whether we categorize it as good or bad—as something that can cause loss of control. This provokes primal fears, even turning it into a survival issue: fight or flight. And if that sounds a little dramatic for everyday workplace change, it remains true that the brain runs all new experiences through its self-protection circuit, trying to determine if it should send some fear or loss signals to get your attention.

Studies show that when we find out something novel is on the way—a new boss, an altered industry requirement, a changed product line, a reorganization—the brain begins searching its memory banks for clues about what might be forthcoming.

Somewhere in our brain is the memory of every experience, emotion, and feeling we have ever had. Labeled *good* or *bad*, *easy* or *hard*, *try to forget*, *try to remember* —they are all in there. Like the stuff in our garage, we can't seem to find resourceful past information when we need it. At times, our memories can be faulty, and we remember things as better or worse than they actually were. Sometimes this distortion can be an advantage, providing confidence to take on a challenge. Other times it is a distraction, a deterrent, an obstacle, even a source of damaging (mis)information.

Consider the following example. A change initiative is announced: as part of a new reporting system, the sales force will have to immediately begin coding orders by region and customer instead of date. If the system implementation has been going well, people are likely to believe that this step will also go as planned. If the system start-up has been a rocky road, additional steps will be construed as potential problems as well. If there is no history to the start-up, then we revert back into our memories to a time we experienced something similar—not necessarily the same, but akin to what we perceive or interpret is happening now. If that memory is positive or resourceful, we are bent in that direction. If not, we are more likely to project the past frustrations, disappointments, and resentments into the present.

Cognitive psychologists call this *schema*, and it is the brain's way of looking for patterns so we can find and act on similarities. One of our central missions in this book is to help you become aware of your work and change schemas, and to show you ways to productively reshape old schemas and create new ones that have improved utility.

Note from Lillie
"If the Shoe Fits"

As mentioned above, both our memories and our personalities have a critical bearing on how we feel, think, and behave in change. Our dominant personal tendencies and communication styles surface as we move through the six stages of The Change Cycle. This helps account for the differences in shades of emotion and in the amount of time it takes people to move through the stages, even with core commonalities in the ways we all process change.

In the Personalities in Change chart on page 13, we map out four distinct personality types and suggest the kind of shoe this person "wears" as he or she journeys through change. Take a look and see if you recognize

Personalities in Change Chart

Shoe	Description	Strengths	Challenges
Hiking Boot	• Conscientious—sometimes at own expense • Builds consensus • Works hard to produce what co-workers need	• Durable; labors through distractions • Values high quality • Desires the simple truth	• Neglects own concerns • Fears being inadequate • Under-uses influence
Cross Trainer	• Charming, visionary, persuasive • Adaptable • Appreciates people and solutions	• Innovative and optimistic • Decisive • Positive influence on others	• Impulsive • Lacks follow-through • Often critical of others
Flip-Flop	• Values diversity, loves a challenge • Social • Easy-going and fun-loving	• Cares about relationships • Team Player • Spontaneous and eager	• Takes on too many projects • Avoids conflict • Takes things personally
Wingtip	• Needs full picture to move forward • Plays by the rules • Uses internal criteria to determine "the truth"	• Thorough and investigative • High attention to standards and details • Analytical	• Hesitant to ask for help • Need lots of proof • Difficulty hearing other points of view

yourself—in part or in full. Also, I hasten to point out that each of these personality types, each "shoe," has particular life and workplace strengths. But no matter which shoe you think fits, you're not simply at its mercy. There are things you can work on, refine, improve. You can make the most of your particular strengths, and team with people who bring other strengths and skills to the table. In looking at this personality chart, you can begin the work of self-awareness and self-knowledge that is so vital to progressing through The Change Cycle.

P.S.: Just in case you're wondering whether Ann and I have done our own self-assessment with help from this chart, the answer is yes. One of us is a perennial cross trainer, the other splits time between being a hiking boot and a flip-flop, depending on the weather.

The Change Cycle

Hoping to find answers to our many questions about the human experience of change, we have traversed up and down the stacks of more than one research library. Albert Einstein said, "If we knew what we were doing, it wouldn't be called Research." We found plenty of data—mountains, even—from fields such as psychology, neurology, physiology, even physics. A lot of it was interesting, much of it even fascinating, but the technical language and detail made it less than fully useful for the average change sufferer. So we cut, pasted, and condensed our findings into the more easily understood and practical Change Cycle model. You are very welcome!

When you look at The Change Cycle model, located on the inside cover, you'll notice it is a circle. This represents the true cyclical (versus linear) nature of each change we experience. In the outside ring are the six sequential and predictable stages of change. The names of the stages (Loss, Doubt, Discomfort, Discovery, Understanding, and Integration) indicate the primary experience of that stage. The inside pie pieces list the thoughts, feelings, and behaviors most associated with that stage. The point is to progress from stage to stage in order to eventually integrate the change experience.

Notice that The Change Cycle uses the colors of a traffic light to signal that the stages mirror the actions we often take at traffic lights. For example, we put ourselves at risk if we don't stop at a red light, just as we do if we fail to stop and deal effectively with the experiences of Stages 1 and 2. The yellow light means caution, and some of us take that to mean slow down and stop, while others hit the gas and speed through. There is no wrong answer here—what do you do at a yellow light? In yellow Stages 3 and 4, caution is in order, and it determines how we experience the challenges of motivation and making choices. At a green light, we move through freely, with little risk. So it is with green Stages 5 and 6. At this point, we should be able to move more easily as we fully assimilate the change and complete the cycle.

We do know that when confronted with change, everyone goes from stage to stage in order. The Change Cycle model is the map that depicts our human experience of each stage of change. This is to say that change is an experience that activates a whole series of predictable and sequential responses as the brain works to equip us to make good choices and sound decisions for the new experience. What we do not know is how long a person may spend in each stage, or how intense the experience might be. None of the stages are considered "good" or "bad," and there are skills that a person can develop to help progress through the stages. And oddly enough, you never need to "like" the change to advance all the way to Stage 6. Understanding how each stage works helps you distinguish the change forest from the trees—a big-picture view that can get you from bitter to better, or from wherever you are emotionally at journey's start, to the end.

The Six Stages

The Red Stages: Loss and Doubt

Why do so many of us have a seemingly instinctive resistance to change?

That was one of the questions that led to the work that anchors this book. In the beginning, we were looking for solutions to ease the stress and loss of productivity caused by corporate change: mergers, acquisitions, downsizing, and the like. What we discovered early on was that people react and respond to change not as employees, managers, spouses, siblings, partners, friends, parents, but rather as human beings. And there are commonalities—essential human patterns—to the ways we react.

Two more questions at the start of our "change curiosity" were:

- Are there common triggers that interfere with people's ability to understand and to take action concerning the changes they face?

- Could a more systematic approach to dealing with life's changes assist people in how they manage variables and how they act during a transition?

The answer to both questions, we found, was yes.

When working with organizations in the midst of change, it is common to hear employees at all levels wishing another part of the organization would "get fixed" and that the change process would be smoother, easier, better. Managers want workers fixed, employees want management fixed—you get the picture. The bottom line is that every level of an organization can become more change-resilient, just as every individual at every level can. As human beings, we are self-correcting, once we know the way.

Self-correcting up to a point, that is. There are reflexes and nonconscious concerns—the triggers mentioned in the bullet point above—that come alive during a change situation, no more so than right at the beginning. The good news is, the more you know about these triggers—the things that impede acceptance and understanding of a change—the faster you can get out of the first two stages, *Loss* and *Doubt*, and the more freedom you create for yourself to act in a way that moves you through the change process.

But at the outset—when the change hits—you actually don't want to try and "move" too much or even "do" too much. You might move (some even run) in the wrong direction. You've barely begun to process the new information, and your decision-making mechanism—your compass; your inner GPS—is not yet sitting squarely in its housing. Hence the "red" stages—red as in stop sign, as in the color of the traffic light. Your work-life has just changed. Life has just changed. Don't try and run the red. Decelerate. Press the brakes. Stop at the intersection. Look left and right. A change can put you in a "fight or flight" mode. You want to do neither.

The light is red. Wait till it is safe to go.

Stage 1: Loss to Safety

We arrive in Stage 1 because our work-life has become different in some way. Maybe something is lost—a job, a promotion, a client. Maybe something is new—a boss, a project, a transfer. Change is standard equipment in any of those scenarios. The primary experience of Stage 1 is loss of control. And either consciously or nonconsciously, our thoughts become cautious; we experience feelings of angst, maybe even fear. Our behavior gets paralyzed.

Even a perceived "good" change, if it is of significant scope, can evoke these responses. This first stage can be a difficult one, because like driving in fog, what you know about the road ahead is equaled by what you don't know, and yet, for your own safety, you have to keep moving. It is important to acknowledge, not ignore or deny, your losses and concerns. Your priority in Stage 1 is to find personal safety—to regain a sense of control.

Key questions to answer: "How am I going to be affected?" "What's the worst that can happen?" "Can I handle that?"

Stage 2: Doubt to Reality

Stage 2 finds us experiencing doubt and a disquieting sense of uncertainty. Doubt is the brain's way of slowing us down, even stopping us from taking action, until more relevant information is gathered. Doubt often triggers defensive behavior as a way of maintaining control. This can lead to varying degrees of resentment, skepticism, and resistance that are counterproductive at best and in some cases even harmful. Stage 2 can cause you to ignore the obvious and only see the picture your way, causing you to defend your view of the situation as if it were The Truth. Job 1 in Stage 2 is to move past fictions and step into reality.

Stage 2 can be dramatic in organizational change because emotions run high, and anger, accusations, and varying levels of mistrust surface to drive and distort communication. More often than not, there will be a sizable number of people within the organization who will use blame and who will fight to prove that "their way" or the "old way" is still better. They argue, lobby, protest. But change is not fair, even if we beg, demand, plan, or wish it to be. Stage 2 is the soapbox for organizational change complaints, home to currently running soap operas like *The Change and the Restless*, *All My Changes*, and *As the Change Turns*.

The Yellow Stages:
Discomfort and Discovery

As in the world of your commute or drive to the grocery store, the color yellow in The Change Cycle means that you should exercise a little caution. You're not on the open road yet. It's not time to click on cruise control. You've got traffic, a cross street, a car waiting to turn left in front of you. Whether you're a "step on it" type behind the wheel or someone who slows down when you see yellow (you know who you are!), in the world of work changes, beating the light is not really an option. There's a limit to your powers of acceleration.

Nor would you want to floor it, even if you could. You're still getting your bearings, you don't quite see the way clear yet. There's still some mental fog.

Better things are ahead, but you're not quite sure how to get there yet.

Stage 3: Discomfort to Motivation

Stage 3—*Discomfort*—is characterized by anxiety, confused thoughts, and feelings of being overwhelmed. Together they add up to sluggish behavior. Here, we wait while the brain works to assimilate—to organize, categorize, and put language on the new change picture.

We feel informed but disjointed, and there is a natural tendency for productivity to drop and for even the normally well-organized person to become absent-minded, lethargic, "off their game." This can be a frustrating stage because by now employees have clarity about the change and what it will ultimately mean for them. Absenteeism is often high during this time. Planning for this predictable "slow-down" period is imperative, a smart investment for any organization.

To break through, to move forward, in Stage 3, you need to decide on small steps to take and make a concerted effort to reengage your motivation and keep it sustained.

Those who can't find motivation? They may stall, even backslide. They've entered . . . "The Danger Zone."

Stage 4: Discovery to Perspective

Issues in the first three stages were "problems to solve." Here in Stage 4, *Discovery*, there are "solutions to implement." Perspective—moving beyond constrictive thinking—is the reward in this stage. Your energy comes back. Your concentration returns. Your challenge is to take the created options, and make choices and decisions about the next best steps. A broader vision, a renewed decisiveness, bring a sense of control and optimism.

In Discovery, you learn to entertain opposing views as a way to widen your work and life lens. You search out optimal choices, eyes on both present and future.

The Green Stages:
Understanding and Integration

Understanding and *Integration* are what you have been moving toward, the reason for your work of self-understanding and self-assessing. Understanding will have you doing some calm looking back at your change experience in order to glean insights to use down the road. That's not all that happens here, of course, but it is part of it. The

Integration stage is where wisdom comes into play, and you find yourself looking into the future of your work and life with a cheering clarity of vision.

In these last two stages, you place a few final pieces into the change jigsaw puzzle and all at once you are looking at the complete image. No more hesitation or cautious looking left-right as the light is green and you zoom onward.

Stage 5: Understanding the Benefits

As we identify the benefits of the change, both short-term and long-term, our behavior becomes more insightful—and more pragmatic. We feel we finally have a good understanding of things. We've learned what it takes to make this change work, we've learned about ourselves; we've learned lessons that will be of use in the next work or life change. In this heightened "learning mode," we find ourselves wanting to take in as much newness, as much information, as we can absorb, both at work and outside work. We're confident. Productive.

To move on, we reflect on the deeper meaning of the change and the change process.

Are we "happy" in Stage 5? We might be. It depends on the change. As with all of the stages, this one can involve things we wish were otherwise. And of course some changes will never be completely reconciled, neatly packaged, or fully accepted. At times, crisis, chance, or nature force us to endure events that cannot be "managed well"—in any way—by anybody. Layoffs, downsizing, mergers, transfers, bankruptcy, project failures, burnout—and that is just at work. Change is not always easy or pretty. Life is a messy, mysterious, eventually fatal business, yet in Stage 5, we accept and understand that, like it or not, somehow we go on.

Stage 6: Experiencing Integration

Here we fully integrate our change experience into our life—at work and at home. Emotionally, we experience empathy and often find ourselves freely offering assistance to others who may not be as far along in the process. We feel a renewed confidence in our ability to flexibly adjust to the next round of changes life will bring. In Stage 6 people speak of having crisp focus and feeling contentment. Stage 6 challenges include avoiding ego and complacency, and elevating understanding into wisdom.

You've gone from "survive" to "thrive." You have insight into the ramifications, consequences, and rewards of the change—and you can clearly assess past, present, and future.

When whole organizations can consistently move to Stage 6, they are successful beyond the marketplace. They count—to their communities, their customers, their vendors, their stakeholders. "The Change" isn't a big transition anymore; it's simply the *status quo*.

When people can consistently move to Stage 6, they deepen their change resiliency, they're flexible through uncertainty, they move closer to their larger work and life goals.

The Change Cycle Stage Profiles chart on page 25 captures the essence of this stage—and the five that came before it. Use it for a quick and concise guide to The Change Cycle basics.

Change 101

Change comes in all shapes, sizes, and intensities. It happens to all of us. Sometimes it sneaks up on us, sometimes it hits us over the head, sometimes we are lucky enough to choose when and how it happens. And it always happens. Growing up, we all needed a Change 101 class. This book is that class. No spitballs.

The Change Cycle Stage Profiles

Change Cycle Stage	Objective	Challenge	Key Question	Exit Strategy
Stage 1: Loss	To acknowledge losses and concerns	Channel fear into appropriate action	What is the worst that could happen?	Create **safety** for yourself and the organization
Stage 2: Doubt	To face reality by letting go of fiction	Manage anger, both passive and aggressive	What are the facts and who can give them to me?	Seek valid and accurate **information**
Stage 3: Discomfort	To breakthrough instead of breakdown	Take small steps despite frustration	Which steps can I take to expedite a breakthrough?	Focus on finding the **motivation** to keep yourself moving
Stage 4: Discovery	To gain perspective that comes from looking at all sides	Consider productive options without getting stuck	How can I determine the next best step to take?	Make **decisions** that reflect my ability to see the best options
Stage 5: Understanding	To grasp the meaning of this change in a deeper way	Enjoy greater understanding while knowing that you are not finished yet	What have I learned that can increase my productivity?	Identify the **benefits** in order to begin integration
Stage 6: Integration	To make the change a natural part of your life	Create stability while warding off complacency	How can I help those who are not as far along?	**Integration**

Chapter One

What's the Worst That Could Happen?

It is not the strongest of the species that survives, nor the most intelligent, but rather the one most responsive to change.

Charles Darwin

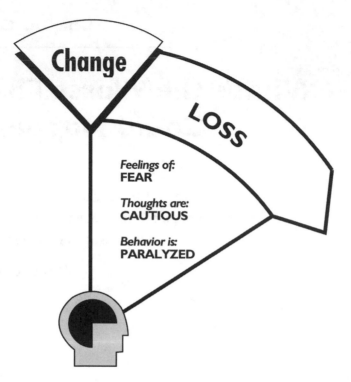

Stage 1: Moving from Loss to Safety

Let's say you arrive at work one day and are stunned by an announcement that your boss has abruptly quit for personal reasons. Data shoots from your brain's memory banks to (supposedly) help you deal with this news. After those initial emotional, internal comments (such as *Hooray!* or *Oh no!*), you very quickly get to the business of how exactly this is going to affect you. Welcome to Stage 1, Loss (and Loss of Control).

In Stage 1, you are dealing with the knowledge that, for better or worse, to a greater or lesser degree, life at work has changed or will change. You have lost or are going to lose something: even if it is simply *the way things were*. And chances are, this change will involve a loss of control for some duration—or at least it will create the fear that control will be lost. Faced with this situation (whether the change is big, with bomb-like impact, or minor), most human beings react in the same way on some level. We feel concern about what might come. We start calculating the potential impact on our particular work-life (and life beyond work). And, no matter our sophistication, part of us kicks into "survival mode." The thought of the unfamiliar is the trigger.

Obviously "change-bombs" are going to—and *should*—engage our survival instincts more deeply than the less dramatic stuff (the difference, say, between getting pink-slipped and learning your division is scheduled for three days of "retraining"), but people being people, word of a change always engages the part of the brain that, in the evolutionary sense, has been around the longest: the more instinctive, less analytic, part.

So know to expect some visceral reactions at the start. There will likely be more emotion than analysis in your initial response. The picture you form of what's to come may not be what's to come. Be patient with yourself. Don't ask too much of yourself. You're at an intersection. Take a breath. Look around. Just as traffic lights go from red to green, you'll get through the change. People do.

Hello Change, Goodbye Control

If you're reading this chapter as an employee, what we present in these pages can help you deal with the newness and the impact of your change by suggesting what to expect in your reactions and by giving you tools to self-assess, self-monitor, self-challenge, and self-teach. Management can do things to properly announce and implement a change; with self-awareness, you can increase the amount of responsibility you take for managing the change at the levels of your duties and work spirit.

If you're reading this as a manager or leader, the over-arching point is that during the introduction of a change your employees will find themselves in an emotional place (as you might yourself). And this may or may not be out-wardly apparent (often it is apparent: on faces, not to mention the groan from the back of the room). At any rate, it's unlikely the change will be received with the logic of *Star Trek*'s Mr. Spock. We're only human. And you as a manager/leader are at a critical moment, perhaps *the* critical moment, because what is done during the announcement of a change conditions employee attitudes and immediately gets them assessing (often with feeling) what it means for them professionally and personally. If management hypes the change as "Great!" and "Good for everyone!" while stated concerns and questions get ignored or shrugged off, employees can go negative fast and slide toward inertia. It is much better to be open and realistic about the change, acknowledging ramifications good and bad, listening to objections, and validating concerns (and there will be concerns).

How We Feel in Stage 1: Fearful

Warning—the F-word cometh. No, not that one. *Fear.* There is some of it in Stage 1. There is more of it in some people than others, obviously. And certain changes create more fear than others. But it is unrealistic—it is inaccurate—to believe that workplace change, at the outset, arrives in a fear-free package. Novelty and the perceived loss of control engage the survival part of the brain, the one where fear (and friend's angst and concern) resides. Its purpose is to get our attention—to tell us a situation is fluid. Things could change for the bad; they could change for the good. But right now, we don't know which. Right now, we're out of our comfort zone. How do we get back there? This chapter has tips to get you started.

According to the great mid-twentieth-century psychologist Abraham Maslow, people's greatest need after those that assure basic survival (water, food, and shelter, not to mention chocolate and ESPN) is *safety*—not only physical but emotional. When our sense of safety and control is threatened, we go into the "fight or flight" mode. We enter this mode quickly, unconsciously. The twenty-first-century workplace is a long way from the plains and caves of our ancient ancestors, but we share with these forebears some of the same basic needs and some of the same basic responses. It's built-in wiring.

What does this "early-brain" thinking mean for the workplace? It means, not to put too fine a point on it, that companies and organizations need to anticipate the full range of responses that follow a change announcement, including people feeling removed from all things safe.

For employees, the first challenge is to use awareness to address what you are feeling. From here you can start the process of distinguishing between fears pointing to things that truly require your attention and those fears that are unfounded, distracting, fanciful.

As you consider the change, ask yourself, *What's the worst that could happen?* Then ask, *Could I live with that?* In many cases of organizational change, people find they can answer yes to the second question. That puts a box around a Stage 1 fear. Go on to remind yourself that worst-case scenarios usually remain at the level of "scenario."

How We Think in Stage 1: Cautiously

When you experience a change, your brain sends caution signals. This can be positive. Caution helps you assess before you act—it supports you in watching for decision-making traps and decoys. Cautious thoughts are questioning thoughts, and this is a time when information and answers are needed.

When caution hangs around too long, however, it hardens into suspicion (or worse, paranoia). Everyone knows someone in an office or organization with a persecution complex. According to this person, people are always out to get him or her, even the maintenance guy who seemed to take "unusually long" in coming by with his ladder and light bulbs to change the overhead light.

Needless to say, this individual is a manager's delight during a time of change. (Not.)

So understand that in Stage 1 your thoughts will be cautious—no two ways about it—but keep your self-assessment unit running, because caution can shade into something overly fearful and suspicious during the uncertainty of company change. After a certain point, extended caution just means you are in a rut, unable to navigate the change.

How We Act in Stage 1: Paralyzed

There's not a lot of action in Stage 1. In fact, our behavior can become more or less frozen, with all attention going to the change and with apprehension perhaps holding us in place.

A better kind of stillness would be a "pause"—a pause to assess, a reflective balance in that initial phase after a workplace change is announced. But to expect that you will react with considered poise or alternatively to "hit the ground running" right after a change is introduced is usually not realistic.

Better to be temporarily stalled, though, than to strike out rashly or to head for the hills.

To Know More, Notice More

The following behaviors and attitudes indicate someone struggling with Stage 1:

▽ Withdraws—avoids talking about thoughts and feelings

▽ Concentrates on old routines, dodging the change

▽ Speculates about results that have been his or her experience in the past

▽ Perceives a large or total loss of control over the situation

▽ Focuses on self, with little or no focus on the organization

▽ Acts powerless in the face of the change

▽ Fights the change, freezes, or puts up defenses

One Company, Different Perspectives

Often the difference between what is "said" when a company initiates change versus what is "heard" leaves executives, managers, and workers at an impasse. Consider the varying perspectives. Executives consider issues as they relate to the stakeholders—the customer, employees, management, vendors, stockholders, the market. Managers are responsible for taking tasks to completion and managing productivity and quality regardless of extenuating circumstances. Employees are at the far end of the information chain. They get the bottom-line information, but they are often left without specifics concerning the change, including the why, what, how, and when. This puts them into "The Change Cycle." Presented with the change, it often doesn't take much for employees to feel a loss of control.

Performance expectations are high and morale is low. The "old system"—a cause of much employee frustration in recent history—looks great compared to changing to something new and unproven. *The tug of war between the old way and the new way has begun.* The implementation plan moves forward nonetheless. Deadlines must be met.

In Stage 1, these concerns must be addressed—by both management and employees. Employees must take responsibility and realize they are employed in an evolving workplace that will continually upgrade systems, policies, and procedures. Management must be committed to providing workers with the best and most timely training and skills-enhancement possible to keep staff successful in the workplace. Stage 1 sometimes makes the change seem as if management is pitted against those they manage. It's hard to believe that a new system will be your light at the end of the tunnel when you are sitting in the dark.

Case in Point: Creativo Plus Inc.

No one is exempt from Stage 1, not employees, managers, or the CEO. Yet the intensity and time spent there can vary greatly depending on the individual. What may seem an insignificant change to one person could have a profound effect on another. Example: Creativo Plus Inc. is adding a second shift to its production schedule. Management has announced that all employees will rotate through the new shift one week per month for six to twelve months as production needs are determined and new hiring can take place.

When the addition of the second shift was announced, employee reaction was by and large positive. The need for the company to add production time was a victory of sorts for everyone. It meant demand for its products was increasing, and the value of the company and the employees' part in it was growing. Yet that growth came with a price that became an intrusion and, in some cases, a real problem in certain people's personal lives. As a peacekeeping strategy, the company added an hourly bonus for these second-shift hours. Unfortunately, that has not fully addressed the situation for some employees.

Sam has been a loyal employee for over nine years. He is well liked and easy to work with. But now the attitude of this once consistently good performer has shifted. His productivity has dropped, his demeanor soured. His manager is at a loss as to what is going on. Sam has been quiet and brooding since the second-shift announcement, and when asked what is wrong, he replies, "Nothing." Sam's story is typical of the ripples caused by changes at work that can affect an employee's personal life as well:

> On Tuesday and Thursday evenings, I coach youth sports at my church. One night it's my daughter's team and the other for my son. As a divorced dad, this is an important and special time with my kids. We had a long and hard custody and visitation battle. Finally it all seems to be working for us, and now I'm really concerned that the addition of the second shift will cause big problems for me with my ex-wife.

To the surprise of her manager, Jan, too, is upset with the second-shift schedule. Jan has always been willing to work a couple of hours overtime, claiming the extra money came in handy. Her boss thought she would be happy with the added financial incentives and was caught off guard when Jan pleaded to be excluded from the rotation. This single mother of three school-age children tells her story:

> Having an opportunity to make extra money working overtime is always appealing, but I can only do it when I can get my mom to watch my kids after school. Working the second shift is actually going to

cost me money after I pay a babysitter—if I can find someone reliable one week per month who will work nights. They're really good kids, but evenings at home are chaotic with homework and school projects. I'm worried sick about going for a whole school week with very little or no time with my children. They need me.

Neither Sam nor Jan is behaving like a victim of the new schedule—they aren't the types to play the victim, no matter the difficulty—but they're stuck in Stage 1, feelings apprehensive, thoughts cautious, behavior, if not paralyzed, at least limited.

Their colleague Andrew is up against more—much more. Two weeks after the shift-change announcement, he learned he was being terminated. With production quotas rising, his work performance, the least impressive in his unit, came into even sharper relief. The news wasn't a total surprise, as he'd been on a kind of "probation," but still, to let him go at a time of new hiring came as a shock. With child support, a mortgage, and a load of credit-card debt, Andrew has been driving a cab along with his Creativo job to make ends meet. But the moonlighting left him exhausted during his day job—something had to give.

I should have stopped driving the cab. I didn't love my job at Creativo, but at least it had health insurance. And a steady paycheck. The first two nights after getting the termination news, the only thing I was good for was sitting in my house, watching TV or staring into space. I couldn't sleep. I couldn't bring myself to drive the cab. I'm telling myself that now I have my reason to do the thing I've been wanting to do for a long time, and that's move to Alaska. I have a couple friends up there. But right now it's hard to think about the future. It's weird: even when you've been warned something like this might happen, it's another thing to actually get the news. I need to come up with a new plan.

The Only Way Out Is Through

The magnitude of Andrew's change is obviously far more severe than what Sam and Jan are dealing with. From a financial angle especially, his grounds for fear are substantial. He is facing a great deal of unknown. There is loss, and then there is Loss. That said, the three workers share one thing: they are all in the early stages of The Change Cycle and will need to take similar internal steps to move forward. Sam's and Jan's fears are family fears— a threat to the delicate weaves of parenting and domestic life. They wouldn't want to change places with Andrew, but their fears are also real and need addressing.

Learning Curves

How you and those you work with talk about the change, including the way you "talk" to yourself (that internal conversation always running in our heads), is not just "words, words, words," to borrow a line from Shakespeare. What you "say"—aloud or internally—impacts how you interpret the change situation and also gives clues to the way you are dealing with it, in both conscious and nonconscious ways.

Are you or those you work with making any of the following comments?

▽ "Why?" and "Why me?"

▽ "I'm afraid of what this might mean."

▽ "I am going to keep doing things the way I've always done them."

▽ "This is just another fad."

▽ "I don't know who to believe."

▽ "What have I done to deserve this?"

▽ "They don't care about us."

▽ "Why will this work any better than other things we have tried?"

You'll have to change your mind before you change your tune, but paying attention to the talk (outer and inner) builds another level of awareness—always a good thing.

Stage 1 Priority: Creating a Sense of Safety

To move out of Stage 1, you need to feel some degree of control over the situation and have a sense that your safety is not threatened. Until this happens, we have a tendency to take one step forward and two steps back with each new tidbit of information or new experience during the change. What do control and safety mean in your particular work situation? We all have standards—minimums for the specific arena of our work lives.

Precisely defining the change in a way that allows you to summarize what it is in a sentence and how it will affect you both now and during the next three to six months will help add to your sense of control. The clarity you'll gain will assist you in differentiating between legitimate fears and ungrounded fears, the latter perhaps clouding your thinking as you strive to find your new work footing and direction. With every imagined fear you eliminate, you improve your perspective and make your situation feel a little less threatening.

Pinpointing the Change

Many of us tend to generalize situations. In the uncertain and uneasy state of mind that is Stage 1, this is not always a good thing. The "Pinpointing the Change" exercise that follows is designed to assist you in determining if you generalize like this, or, alternatively, if you cling to specific details of a change, potentially ignoring the real issues driving your thoughts, feelings, and behaviors. Pinpointing helps you gain a sense of control over a situation or issue that may be gripping you—consciously or not.

As you will see in the example, once you have clarity about the change, you might be surprised to find that by dealing with the most worrying issue, other concerns tend to diminish. When you clarify the issues as best as you can at this early point in the crisis or change, you will have a good indication of what's what. Being able to focus on some specific aspect of the change situation will give you perspective and allow you to move more quickly through your transition. After all these years, we still use this quick and easy pinpointing exercise to gain clarity and make sure we are dealing with the real issue.

"Pinpointing the Change" Exercise

Martin is worried. He knows that if his marketing plan fails, he will have no one to blame but himself. But he can't seem to get a grip. He feels inundated by problems at work and the financial stresses they have caused at home. Right now it feels as if he has no alternatives—he fears he's lost in a lose-lose situation. He can't sleep, he's irritable, and his co-workers seem to be avoiding him. One thing he could do is sit down with a pen and paper and take a moment to pinpoint his change. His questions and answers might look like this:

A. Name a significant change you are experiencing now:
Potential failure of the new marketing campaign

B. What specific losses does it create for you?
- *Loss of feeling competent as a marketing manager*
- *Project financial bonus, which we desperately need*
- *My boss's confidence in me for big projects*

C. Which loss is most uncomfortable for you right now?
Project financial bonus, which we desperately need

D. Why? What specifically makes it uncomfortable?
I counted on this project's success to ease our financial situation at home

E. Restate your change to more specifically reflect what you are thinking and feeling now.
I am feeling like a failure, afraid that there will be no financial bonus

Notice how the example started with naming the change: *Potential failure of the new marketing campaign.* That's the factual element. It ended with *I am feeling like a failure, afraid that there will be no financial bonus.* That is the issue. Sometimes the facts and issues have an interesting relationship with each other; other times they have no relationship or common ground at all. It is easier to name the fact, but it's the issue that requires attention. Why? Because, as in Martin's case, it is the issue driving thoughts and behavior in Stage 1.

Case in Point: DATAs Group Inc.

DATAs Group Inc. had announced via company intranet and a public press release that they were installing a somewhat controversial new software program for use company-wide. Rumors had been plentiful and information sketchy as to the details, expectations, and timing of the implementation.

Talk on the grapevine was that many employees in the accounting and finance departments would lose their jobs through reassignment, but not necessarily lose their employment. Morale was sinking, and productivity along with it. On the insistence of the site-management team, the executive leaders decided that to ensure employee buy-in of the new system, the president would hold a meeting for the members of the finance and accounting departments to clarify the impending changes.

At first, Sue Martin, vice-president for human resources, was thrilled that the senior leaders were showing an interest in a grassroots communication plan for the employees. That was short-lived after she attended the planning session dictating the president's intention and communication format.

He had decided on a "town hall meeting" format, and because of lack of space on-site he rented the community theater several blocks from the company building. The plan called for the 180 employees to walk to the theater, where a jazz band would be providing entertainment and company logo-wear would be given away in the lobby. The president would then update everyone on the implementation time frames and goals, in addition to the objectives and expectations of the roll-out. His intention was to "sell" the many qualities of the new program and then answer questions from the audience.

Sue opposed this plan. She clearly and succinctly pointed out the flaws and landmines in his approach, and she calmly built consensus about why a different communication style needed to be utilized and what specifically needed to be done, by whom, and how.

Using The Change Cycle model, she explained that management's position of "This change is good for the company" was coming from a Stages 5 and 6 mentality that would be neither appreciated nor supported until employees had moved out of red Stages 1 and 2. The changes were certain to upset many long-tenure employees. Sue predicted, however, that within the next several months the system changes would be embraced and praised. Until then, what is perceived as good for the company and what is perceived as good for the employees may be quite different and would take time to get in sync.

The bottom line? Employees should not be expected to show enthusiastic support at the time of the initial announcement—they need time to assess their control factors and gain an accurate picture of the impact the change will have on them as individuals and in their intact work teams.

Sue praised the idea of going to the theater: a good neutral, comfortable, and convenient place. But she opposed the jazz band, explaining that a festive atmosphere would not sit well with employees who were going to be negatively affected by the change (or perceived they would be). She also suggested dropping the idea of giving away logo-wear. The demographics of the employee group were more than 70% women, and baseball caps and t-shirts were an unlikely incentive to get them to buy into the changes. And her firmest point was that the president should not answer questions from the audience, pointing out that employees would ask him operations-driven questions he had little or no chance of answering correctly. After a lengthy and at times heated discussion, Sue prevailed on all points.

On the day of the meeting, Sue acted as moderator. She welcomed everyone and clearly and concisely explained what the meeting's format would be. She invited them to ask questions, explaining that queries would be keyed into a computer and shown on a screen above the stage before being answered via e-mail within a week. She then introduced the president, and he made his comments. Then questions began appearing on the screen. There were a lot of them—seventy-four to be exact. The president started sweating after about the ninth question: it was a good thing he wasn't being asked to answer them. When the questions stopped, Sue thanked the employees, and they quietly got up and walked out.

The president admitted he was relieved it was over. He thanked Sue for using her leadership and management skills to turn what could have been a disaster into a successful interaction with the employees and a valuable lesson for him. He acknowledged that her insistence to build rapport and not try to fix or oversell the change honored what the employees were experiencing—the loss of control synonymous with Stage 1. He admitted that his plan to secure employee support would have backfired no matter what he could or would have offered as incentives to support the changes.

During the following week, the employee questions that could be answered were answered, and the issues that required more attention were handled in a variety of ways, including focus groups and system-review teams. Feedback about the meeting praised the style and format as the best possible way to have received the information, and employees gave the president high marks for his attitude and willingness to be up-front and truthful with them.

> Information and communication are not synonyms.
> Information is giving out, while communication
> is getting through.
>
> *S. J. Harris*

Worlds—or at Least Stages—Apart

A central reason change announcements are such a challenge for people in leadership positions is that they may have had weeks, even months, to cycle through the change at the conceptual level and are now delivering news (of new skill requirements, a systems change, culture overhaul, supervision restructuring, a merger, layoffs) to people who very well may be hearing it, at least in fleshed-out, official form, for the first time.

Messengers might be in Stage 5. Their audience? Just now stepping onto a road whose signs say Loss, Fear, Anger, Rejection, Mistrust. *Houston, we have a problem.* Leadership might be ready to go-go-go. They grasp things with green-stage understanding. Employees might very well be experiencing something akin to that moment in cartoons when a character gets steamrolled down to two dimensions and then tries to pop back into shape.

It takes imagination and empathy for leadership to announce and roll out the change in a way that can bridge the stage gap. Without efforts in this direction, employee resentment can set in quickly, with red-stage protraction the result. Employees realize that sometimes unfortunate changes must be made. But if all they're getting from leaders and management is green-stage enthusiasm and way-forward speeches, they'll respond in some basic human ways. Going through their heads, with some frustration and perhaps even bitterness, are things like, *I thought we were doing a good job—you told us so. What I have pride in doing for this organization, you are now saying can be done better elsewhere. I missed my kids' t-ball games, recitals, and birthday parties for this company and this is the reward?*

Executives frame change as innovation, market opportunity, expansion, streamlining—keys to success—whereas employees often talk of IOC ("inevitable organizational change") and think, *Here we go again.* They hear change and think disruption, trouble, threat. They may feel inadequate, undervalued, disposable, "used."

Picture the most chaotic intersection you can imagine. Seven roads intersecting, clusters of traffics lights all over, concrete islands, people driving at all speeds, some cars stalled, pedestrians darting into traffic, and one lone traffic cop. This intersection is a company change going awry, the cop the change leaders. *Officer, please give us a sign!* A bad announcement of change is not the sole cause of company chaos during implementation. But it sure doesn't help. Often the extra costs, lost productivity, and sinking morale during a troubled change (sometimes tempting leaders to call the whole thing off) are not measures of the change's innate worth but indictments of the way the change was revealed to the company and handled at the very start of the process.

A well-done change announcement does the following:

▽ Explains business issues that have made the change necessary

▽ Highlights how the change addresses these issues

▽ Acknowledges the change's upside and downside

▽ Answers why, what, when, and how questions

▽ Acknowledges past difficulties and disappointments

▽ Gives as much overall, big-picture information as possible

▽ Addresses short-, medium-, and long-term ramifications

▽ Offers milestones when possible, instead of hard deadlines

▽ Avoids cheerleading and overselling the benefits

▽ Shows an interest in employee questions, concerns, comments, and the like

▽ Has a follow-up plan for the announcement

None of these elements will work all of the time, but all of them will work some of the time. In a changing environment, people can always deal better with what they know rather than with what they feel compelled to speculate about or invent because of an info vacuum.

Allies, Obstacles

In every stage in The Change Cycle, there are things to welcome, things to avoid, and keys to moving on. Below are entries for Stage 1, drawn from our experiences working with companies and organizations ranging from Honeywell, Nestle, and American Express to the NCAA and the CIA (don't ask). Of course it would be nice if the whole stage could be avoided—loss, fear, shock, bitterness, and all the rest of it. That would be welcome, but unfortunately change doesn't work that way. It works, but not that way.

Things to Avoid in Stage I

▽ **Trying to "fix the change"**

In Stage 1, there is really nothing to fix. You need a little time and stillness while sorting out what is happening. Be patient—with yourself and others.

▽ **Sending a message that the old way was better**

Ask yourself, *When the "old way" you are now lamenting the loss of was the "new way," how did you feel about it then?* Chances are, you hated it. In time, when the change gets more familiar, it will come to seem normal and lose its emotional impact.

▽ **Hyping the change**

Whether you are a worker, manager, or leader, selling the change in a big way can backfire. While processing the reality of "things aren't the way they used to be" and experiencing a loss of control, people can only take so much enthusiasm about the change's "extraordinary benefits." Hype causes others to suspect your motives and wonder if you are trying to take advantage of them instead of dealing with the impact of the change. Everything has positives and negatives— they'll wonder why you're only willing to look at the former.

To Be More Resourceful in Stage 1

▽ **Manage fear**

Let fear work for you, not against. Fear can get your attention, sharpen your senses, and heighten your alertness to current needs. Let it direct your focus to defining your predicament—and a way out. It's the unwarranted fears that cause trouble. Identify one of these, put it in the mental wastebasket, and hit "delete." Eliminating a groundless fear improves your perspective and moves you a step closer to safety.

▽ **Have empathy toward others**

Change has a unique impact on everyone. What may seem like a minor deal to you may be a major deal to a co-worker because he or she cares for an ailing parent, goes to night school, or has childcare responsibilities that you don't know about.

▽ **Listen**

It pays to listen, no matter where you are in the organization. Changes made from a big-picture perspective can sometimes be blind to the impact on operational details. When employees voice concerns, important operational steps can be addressed early on, and resources of time, money, and quality can be saved. And most times it's a positive when employees listen to each other and to voices from higher up the organizational chart. Even if management's communication style might need some work, that doesn't mean what they're trying to convey down the ranks lacks value.

Keys to Moving On

▽ Acknowledge your losses and concerns.

▽ Channel fear into appropriate action.

▽ Ask, "What's the worst that could happen?"

There might be one more key. It's something to avoid. *Avoid believing Stage 1 lasts forever.* It doesn't. People find solutions. People find ways to move on.

Note to Self:

Get safe. Be safe. Stay safe.

Facts Over Fiction

Because things are the way they are,
things will not stay the way they are.

Bertolt Brecht

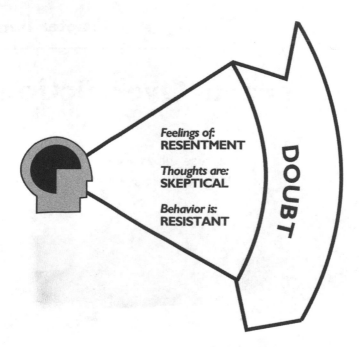

Stage 2: Shifting from Doubt to Reality

The angst and wallop of Stage 1—where the workplace change hits and the familiar is lost or will be lost—give way to resistance, skepticism, resentment, and even anger in the stage that follows. We go from squirrelly to some other animal: a mule, a bull, a squint-eyed cat. We can feel we're being "wrangled" in the wrong direction. Welcome to Stage 2, *Doubt*.

Having established in Stage 1 that the sky is not falling, you're now faced with a new challenge: dealing with your doubts about the change. A lot seems unknown. You might have questions both about the initiative and the

leadership behind it and about the grounds of your own hesitance: an internal tug-of-war. This stage is present— in a big way—in all organizational change, and managing it well is imperative.

The Noise of Stage 2

In Stage 2 emotions run high. Voices can get loud. There might be some harsh words. Okay, there will be harsh words. With blame and anger circulating, communication challenges are as great as they are in Stage 1.

During company change, the workplace becomes a rumor mill. Or it becomes more of a mill than it already is—a thing souped-up, turbocharged. The swirl of talk starts as soon as an inkling of the transition starts reaching people, and it continues on through the change announcement and implementation. In Stage 2, with employees doubting and some resisting, the yakkety-yak can really get cranking—conspiracy theories, hearsay, protests, accusations, arguments, historical references, predictions. Meanwhile, what everyone really needs is for the noise to stop. They want an opportunity to assess their reactions and responses and figure out what information they need, what specific questions to ask.

Knowing that all the hubbub is natural in Stage 2 but not always productive can help you develop a "filter," one aimed at letting in the additional data you need while filtering out the loose talk and speculation. Stage 2 is the soapbox stage: people on their little platforms, filling the air with complaints, counterviews. Between them and the change, a lot is coming at you. Installing your own personal noise-filter is an element of maintaining your boundaries.

Without clear message channels up and down the organization, the emotion that is being released during this stage can become wave-like and work against the change, damaging the work environment, slowing productivity. Some employees dig in their heels, convinced of the rightness of their position. Doubt and change-hindering feelings work overtime. In this second red stage, the company challenge is to make sure red remains a traffic-light metaphor, rather than "code-red."

But there's good news here. Just as fear exists to increase our caution and alertness, doubt is the brain's hard-wired way of slowing us down in an unfamiliar situation so we take time to gather information before acting—it is a hedge against rash action or knee-jerk behavior. Doubt pushes us to dig for the facts behind the evolving scenario. You might have to do a little jujitsu with your doubt, however, turning it to your advantage. How? By recognizing that not only is doubt a natural human state during change—a normal Stage 2 response— but in fact it is delivering an important message.

What's the message saying? *Get more data.* That's a central Stage 2 objective. You want to reach for facts, rather than letting doubt bubble you in and create a state where you believe you alone hold The Truth.

We can say the same for anger. Consider it a form of energy. In Stage 1 the change announcement might have left you numb. Stopped you in your tracks. But now you're feeling something. The blood is starting to flow. Make use of your emotion. Harness it—for motion.

In Stage 2 we change our posture a bit. Instead of feeling as though the change is going to get us, we decide that we are going to get it. Our emotion can fuel our quest. We become more animated. We become another kind of animal. Stage 2 can be a platform enabling you to get a deeper picture of the change (thus creating momentum), or it can turn into a time of conflict and resistance. At the end of the day, the choice is yours.

Your goal is to accentuate fact-finding and discourage the tendency toward blame and defensiveness. Ask yourself: *What kind of information do I need in order to have a full and accurate picture of the change? Would more high-level or conceptual material help? Do I need the thinking behind the change broken into bit-sized chunks? Lots of detail? And how is my need for more information affecting not only my response but the way I process the change for others?*

If you are an employee, be a seeker—of data, of input. If you are a manager or company leader, recognize that clarification of employee roles and responsibilities is often the most overlooked feature on the transition landscape. When change is in the wind, employees immediately begin wondering how their roles and responsibilities will evolve. Clear and regular communication on this front will help minimize employee doubt and resistance.

How We Feel in Stage 2: Resentful

Resentment surfaces in Stage 2. Needless to say, it's not usually a positive. Resentment carries a "me against you" charge. It can take things downhill. Judging the workplace change an inconvenience, an embarrassment, an insult, or an injustice may have grains of truth (maybe many grains) but that ruling is not likely to improve matters. Blaming the boss, the vendor, the new hire, or the regulatory commission, however justified, is not curative. The only thing that counts: *What are you going to do about it now?*

How We Think in Stage 2: Skeptically

We need not be totally skeptical about skepticism. In the same way doubt can be said to have an upside, skepticism helps us test-drive something before we buy it. It helps us check the brakes, it keeps us alert. It's a natural Stage 2 state. Moreover, it can be resourceful if it helps you deepen your analysis, ask good questions, and raise your information standards.

There are two kinds of skepticism. Good skepticism is the *detective* kind. The Columbo kind (or insert TV detective of your choice). The kind that seeks more information, values truth, and is determined to base conclusions only on the gathered evidence. Bad skepticism is the Doubting Thomas (DT) version. A default setting. A broken record. A reflex. No matter what is introduced, as long as it is something new, the DT Skeptic will doubt, resist, and dismiss, and probably complain via his or her megaphone, too. The DT Skeptic becomes part of "the noise."

Your goal is to be a Detective-Skeptic. Even, in a sense, when it comes to yourself. Put that Stage 2 squint to work: consider angles, verify claims. Be wary of assumptions, first takes, conjecture, overreliance on past examples, and the soapbox speechifying of others.

How We Act in Stage 2: Resistant

Stage 2 resistance can come in many forms. It can be external and obvious: an employee shouting during an implementation meeting, or sending e-mails trying to rally supporters to back the "old way," or pointedly slowing down on the job. Or it can be more internal: a less collegial, cooperative attitude in the workplace, perhaps affecting the attitudes of others. Or maybe an employee is taking coworkers aside individually, quietly lobbying.

It could be the resistance is totally inward, even secret—known only to you, the resister. You haven't bought in but are keeping this to yourself. It might be affecting the quality of your work, but since you're being so private, your manager can't do a clear cause-and-effect. The thing is, it's an alienating state. It's messing with your attitude. And since the change is happening whether or not you personally sign on, being inwardly anti-change is not going to get you anywhere.

What about unconscious resistance? Could a person not even be aware that anger or resistance regarding the change has altered his or her work performance or attitude? Most psychologists would say yes. For our part, we'll just say: keep the batteries of your self-assessment charged. Remember to direct that Stage 2 frown at your own thoughts and actions on occasion.

To Know More, Notice More

Here are some behaviors and attitudes that can suggest that you, a coworker, or someone you manage is struggling with this second, doubt-filled stage of The Change Cycle:

▽ Acts defensive—especially of own point of view

▽ Pushes a "me vs. them" dynamic

▽ Shows passive or aggressive anger at decision-makers

▽ Blames others for what is happening

▽ Asks a lot of questions—sometimes the same ones over and over again

▽ Claims not to understand a clear and repeated concept

▽ Works slowly, sluggishly, poorly, or behind schedule

▽ Expresses a lack of trust, even disgust, in facial expressions and body language

And here is some Stage 2 language to listen for:

▽ "There's something they're not telling us."

▽ "How does this affect my job?"

▽ "I don't think we're being treated fairly."

▽ "What do they want us to do?"

▽ "I don't think they understand how things really work!"

▽ "This does not have the benefits they say it does!"

▽ "This will probably be handled just like everything else."

▽ "I don't trust the people making these decisions."

Stage 2: When Open Doors Go Unused

The stew of doubt, anger, and resistance in Stage 2 poses a special problem for middle and lower management, the company's front line for handling all the emotion and changed workplace behavior that a significant transition brings about. Here are some tips for anyone with management responsibilities when workers are in the thick of this difficult stage:

▽ **"Understand that informal invitations such as, "My door is always open if you have questions" may not be appreciated or utilized**
Many employees in Stage 2 don't take the initiative to get "official" answers to their questions. One reason for this is simple: they don't know what they don't know.

▽ **Consistently ask, "What specific information do you want/need?"**
Employees may not always *ask*, but they do appreciate information. Be proactive.

▽ **Be visible—assure others you will share valid information as you can**
Anything you can do to keep employees feeling updated and in the loop is a plus.

▽ **Expect employee skepticism**
Their skepticism is normal. It can be a way of asking for more information.

▽ **Create formal and informal communication systems and follow-up procedures**

Create communication systems that include various written and verbal formats. This helps build trust. Employees closely watch how you handle their questions and concerns.

▽ **Have trained people prepared to deal with conflict** An HR professional trained to deal with conflict resolution is a good Stage 2 resource.

Needed: More Data

Following a corporate merger, Ian, 58, learned he would soon be jobless. To add insult to injury, he was expected to train his replacement. Stunned and despairing, he coped early on by asking those essential first-stage questions, *What's the worst that can happen?* and *Can I live with that?* But in his last weeks on the job, he became angry, resentful, cynical, and skeptical. This state of mind—a bad case of Stage 2—carried over into the weeks after his employment ended.

Luckily the way he conducted himself reflected key early-stage lessons. Even though fuming while training his replacement, he did not have a tantrum or lash out at his bosses, so no bridges were burned in terms of references for any future job. And while buffeted with doubt in those first jobless days (who wouldn't be?), plagued with questions like *How will I pay my bills?* and *Who will hire me at my age?* he did not give in to panic and act impulsively, risking a decision he would regret. Instead, he lived by these smart words: "When in Doubt, Don't."

A variation of this adage is "Don't Just Do Something, Sit There." In other words, before you take some action, make some proclamation, or latch onto a certain view of something, *increase your knowledge base*. Determine the information you need, and find out where to get it. Make a data plan. Ian began to gather his facts. He searched online employment sites, visited a professional recruiter, hired a personal coach, and asked everyone he knew for any information or leads they could share to assist in his job search.

Ian's eagerness to prepare himself for job interviews helped him relinquish his resentment, defensiveness, anger, and blame. He was gradually able to gain a more accurate picture of his future employment chances. He was able to focus on the reality of his new situation. It was this more than anything that reduced his anger. He moved out of Stage 2.

Pinpointing the Point of Resistance

Let's agree that the resisting state of mind is nonideal when it comes to a change at your company or organization—a change with no chance of not happening. What to do? Help yourself get unstuck by posing and answering these questions:

▼ Why am I being resistant?

▼ What specifically am I resisting?

▼ Who am I resisting?

▼ How am I acting my resistance out?

Remember the "Pinpointing the Change" exercise in the previous chapter? Here you are pinpointing the point of resistance. What is at the root of your resistance? Is it concern that the change itself is the wrong one or unwarranted? Is it that you believe the change may make theoretical sense but will be poorly implemented? Is it apprehension that the change, whatever its merits, will cause too much upheaval in your workplace? Are you just tired of change?

Pinpointing aids self-awareness, gives a sense of control, and encourages fact-finding.

The Lure of Speculation

Many of us do a lot of speculating when a situation is new. We find ourselves gaming out all the things that could happen down the road, a fair number of them worrisome. And if unknowns were involved in bringing us to this particular pass, we might speculate about all of them, too. After a certain point (say, the line between analysis and flights of fancy), what we're doing is not helpful. What would help, when you start drawing conclusions based not on evidence but on theories and imagination, would be to hear the booming courtroom voice of television lawyer Perry Mason inside your head: *Your Honor, I object—speculation!*

Perry Mason was before your time? Well, if you channel-surf, you can find him in reruns.

In a workplace-change context, doing your share of speculating can mean that rather than trying to track down more information, you are conducting your own solo (i.e., inside-your-head) investigation into what the company's "true motives" were, the many things that could go wrong if the change doesn't work out, the many ways your life could get lousy fast. Is this helping? Is this a good use of your mental energy? A lot of this kind of speculation can amount to its own form of resistance, and it is usually more trap than tool.

Stage 2 Priority: Getting an Accurate Picture

The key to moving through Stage 2 is being open to finding out the "real deal" behind the change despite our natural tendency to resist the truth of a situation when its newness inspires first fear, then doubt and anger. Mission: discern facts from fiction. It sounds odd to say that doubt and anger could actually help in this process, but properly utilized they can, along with help from an understanding and communicative management team.

In Stage 2, the fog of the first stage starts to lift, and you're ready to process information. Rather than speculating, clinging to your faith in the old way, or becoming part of the misinformation circuit that along with the rumor mill makes Stage 2 a kind of workplace Babel (or high school hallway?), you want to find ... *Just the facts, ma'am.*

Here are some questions designed to assist you in filling information gaps:

▽ What set of facts would help you most?

▽ Where is that information?

▽ Who can help you with your biggest current information question?

▽ Can you obtain it without crossing professional, ethical, or legal boundaries?

▽ Are you trying to find the truth, or further your agenda?

▽ When or how will information be deemed valid by you?

▽ What new behaviors or actions will this information call for?

▽ Are you afraid of the consequences of any information?

▽ Are there any self-imposed obstacles keeping you from getting accurate information?

▽ What question runs through your mind several times each day?

▽ What would you suggest that someone else in your shoes do?

Case in Point: CSC Project

The rumors had been denied for months, but everything had been pointing to the outsourcing of the CSC Project to India. Delays in project updates had stalled the implementation plans at the West Regional Site. The sudden air of secrecy about what was actually happening spoke louder than management probably realized.

As project manager for the implementation team, Drew expected that he would be kept in the loop as new developments affected the project. His management style was open, honest, and direct with his team. Up until the past few weeks, the pressure to keep things moving—on time and under budget—had been intense. Drew had his team's trust, and due to his excellent management skills he was able to keep things on an even keel under the pressure. But then things started to change:

> Literally overnight, the communication from above stopped. My boss denied what was going on, but I started connecting the dots between what had and had not been said, and the picture was ugly. All the time, work, and pride we had put into the development, and now the implementation, appeared to be for nothing—the CSC Project was going to be outsourced. Maybe this was an operational and financial win for the company, but it was a big loss for us at West Regional. I am really angry that this has happened and equally angry about how they communicated why this was such a great decision. What bravado to think that as employees we would cheer for a plan that would cost at least 200 people their jobs. Those 200 people are neighbors and friends. At best, over time, the operations cost savings would be minimal. The numbers being used to justify their actions were faulty. We actually have excellent cost controls here. The cost of the start-up training alone will be staggering.
>
> I resent that our dedication and service to this company is so undervalued that they are willing to spend dollars to save nickels.

Sarah had coordinated vendors at the West Regional Site for as long as anyone could remember. Her negotiating skills combined with her magnetic personality had saved the company hundreds of thousands of dollars over the years. Sarah had built strategic alliances and solid relationships with the vendor companies, and they would do anything for her.

> These past few weeks have been the worst of my career. Every day I get directives from "above" to halt production or stop delivery on some part of the CSC Project, with not one word of explanation. My vendors are panicking and I don't know what to tell them. Surely they wouldn't scrap the CSC Project at this point? We'd lose a fortune settling vendor contracts. I pride myself on being a team player, but I am completely in the dark here and I doubt that anything I say will sound believable to my staff or vendors. I'm trying to just ignore the obvious, but I think the writing is on the wall. I can hardly believe the audacity of management in their internal glad-handing of this new outsourcing deal while denying that they have made us obsolete and likely to be pink-slipped.

Our Power of Self-Assessment

Self-assessment is never easy and is usually less than perfect but it is possible, and it can be both encouraged and improved with time and effort. It is one of our powers as a human being, a defining attribute. So ask yourself: when presented in life with something—large or small— you don't like but can't control, do you tend to flare with anger and look for someone or something to blame, or do you focus on the fact that no matter how much you curse, stomp, and push, a wall is a wall, and your time and energies are best spent elsewhere?

The kinds of people quick to redirect their attention to things they can actually have an effect on tend to carry around less free-floating resentment, and in general these types are slower to experience resentment. But when they do experience it, it may be telling them something. It may be alerting them to the fact that a boundary has been breached. In a workplace context, it can mean, for this person, enough is enough. A line has been crossed. During a time of organizational change, it's important to be open and flexible, but remind yourself that setting professional boundaries is important, too. Know your limits—and yourself. Whole books have been written on what is called "emotional literacy," that ever-valuable ability to read emotions—both those of others and your own, in all their shadings and complexity. People differ in their "reading ability," but with awareness and attention, we can all get better.

Managing Anger

Anger can be the biggest issue we face in Stage 2. Managing it (whether passive or aggressive) is a key challenge in this stage. With a workplace or organizational change can come a reduction in our sense of control, a sense that we're not valued, a sense that we're being victimized, plus embarrassment, frustration, despair. The list goes on. Most of us run through certain patterns of thoughts, feelings, and behaviors when we experience anger. Some of this is basic wiring. But these patterns also have hardened over the years as we have tried to tally what seemed to work and what didn't in situations that triggered anger. As you might imagine, this kind of tallying often falls short of award-winning mathematical precision.

Properly managed, anger can be a catalyst. It's not anger we need to avoid (which is often asking the impossible anyway); it's what we choose to do with it that is important. Where anger causes trouble is when we nurse it internally or go external with it in some out-of-control way. Does a display of anger have the power to change the change? Chances are slim.

Stage 2 is a good time to do some informed stock-taking, a kind of anger inventory. The questions below will help you identify your own anger-patterns, with an eye to upping your power of self-assessment (and hence ability to adapt) when it comes to this potent emotion. Our term "anger strategies" reflects the idea that anger is not purely reactive—an emotion in a vacuum—but rather a situational response developed, for better or worse, over time. Questions to ask:

▽ Do your anger strategies work for or against you?

▽ What specifically works? Why do you think this is?

▽ What doesn't work? Why do you think this is?

▽ Does anger make you feel powerful or out of control? Why?

▽ Do you hold your anger inside, hoping it doesn't "leak out" inappropriately?

▽ Does anger motivate you or frighten you into gathering valid information?

▽ Do you need to upgrade your techniques for managing anger?

▽ What's the first thing you should do differently?

We hope you won't be angry with a bit more on this crucial subject:

Anger Assessment Chart	
Struggling with Anger	**Managing Anger**
What problems does anger create for me?	How can I make my anger work for me?
How do I let my anger take advantage of me?	What is the advantage in being truthful about my angry feelings?
When I get angry, I assume something is bad.	When I feel angry, I assume that there is something I don't know.
Right now, I am paralyzed by my anger.	Will I feel this angry in a week? A month? Tonight?
I often react without thinking.	I gather more information about what's going on.
I blame outside forces, people, and events.	I take responsibility for how I feel.

Rather than stomping your feet, or waving your fist, use your strong Stage 2 emotion to power a data search for change-picture facts. That will get you where you want to go.

Case in Point: The Beeline Company

The Beeline Company proposed a beautiful new headquarters on the outskirts of town. A planning team was formed to disseminate all available information with employees. The team created newsletters, model office designs, charts, and posters. Management was excited, anticipating a favorable workforce response. Though initial reactions had seemed positive, management was surprised and confused by a persistent, underlying attitude of employee resistance. Despite the fact that the move was clearly an upgrade in working conditions for everyone, worker skepticism prevailed. In order to clarify the situation, management disseminated further material about the design of the building. They sat in rooms for hours, trying to determine ways to convince the employees what a good idea the move was. Finally, they decided to have meetings during which employees could ask questions, bring their concerns, or simply voice their opinions.

These meetings gave management a new perspective. The employees voiced clear appreciation for the idea of upgrading their physical working conditions. Yet they also expressed basic, profound concerns. The new location would dramatically affect transportation for some, since public transit was unavailable in that part of town. In addition, many parents utilized the day-care center across the street from the current building, and the relocation would effectively rule that out for most people.

After employees voiced their concerns, management created employee and manager taskforces to study alternatives and propose workable solutions. Once these solutions were available, workers were able to complete their picture of the change and things went smoothly.

Stage 2: "Now It's ... Interpersonal"

Stage 1, with the change-news having just hit, tends to be an inward or personal stage, with everyone dealing in their own ways with serious emotion, some of it—or a lot of it—apprehensive. Personality-wise, the "cross-trainer" often struggles least in this opening stage, drawing on innate resources of positivity and adaptability. It's more "interpersonal" in Stage 2, with people voicing opinions, looking for allies, even getting into conflicts. Here the "flip-flop" and "hiking boot" personalities can be assets, the former easy-going and a peacemaker, the latter a consensus-builder, a dependable colleague. A "wing-tip" person, investigative by nature, needing lots of proof and the full picture (though hesitant to ask for help), will instinctively set about hunting facts—a good thing in Stage 2 (unless it goes on forever).

Things to avoid and welcome reflect the stage's interpersonal dimension.

Things to Avoid in Stage 2

▽ **Getting defensive when people around you are upset, imprecise, or mistrustful**

With the change picture still unclear, those you work with or manage are not always at their best. There's a good deal of self-defending going on—you don't want to add to it. People usually just need more information—no need to take their behavior personally.

▽ **Arguing about what has or has not been communicated**

We vary in what communication formats work best for us. In Stage 2 everyone's still struggling to process the new reality. What you saw in the handout might not be what your coworker "saw." Give help, translate, re-communicate. And seek or provide information in multiple formats and styles: written, oral, visual, formal, informal.

▽ **Ignoring conflict**

Unresolved conflict is a breeding ground for inaccurate information and distrust, keeping people stuck in Stage 2. Facts, truth, and transparency resolve conflicts. Also, don't forget about personality resources—"flip-flops" to the rescue.

Things to Welcome in Stage 2

▽ **Asking for help**

Go to whomever or wherever you need to go to get the facts. If your manager's door is open, walk through.

▽ **Humor**

Humor helps offset and neutralize Stage 2 anger and vociferousness.

How many change agents does it take to change a light bulb?

▽ **Dialogue**

In Stage 2, people want to talk about the change. A lot. A workplace where dialogue is encouraged can help limit the soapbox factor, the Babel of a hundred monologues.

Keys to Moving On

▽ Work through and past your anger.

▽ Ask, "Do I have all the facts?"

▽ View your change in the light of reality.

Learning Curves

If you've done this work of deepening your self-knowledge when it comes to anger strategies, your habits of speculation, and productive skepticism, you have started moving toward clarity. You don't want to stop until you have enough information to form an accurate picture of the change. Hopefully this chapter has helped you accept (or reconfirm) that defensive behavior and reliance on "my position" and "my point of view" declarations don't really move you forward. You might even now have enough data to acknowledge that the change is not all bad and that it could actually do some positive things, even if you do not like it. And you may never like it. The change.

But at least you are seeing it more clearly.

And if you were angry, perhaps you are not as angry now. Maybe only a little less, maybe a lot less. Maybe you are not angry at all. Maybe you were never angry. People are different. But what you have in common with fellow travelers moving out of Stage 2 is that you have a better understanding of the change. This helps your attitude. You may not be cheerleading the change, but you are more accepting of it. At least a little bit. And after the blow of the initial change-news and the emotions of Stages 1 and 2, this can feel like progress.

Note to Self:

Shift happens.

Chapter Three

Taking Charge of Now

Reality is the leading cause of stress among
those of us who are in touch with it.

Jane Wagner

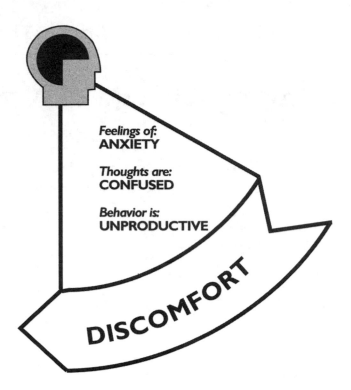

Stage 3: Going from Discomfort to Motivation

It would be great if the arrival of acceptance, in whatever measure, with whatever degree of enthusiasm (or not), was a rocket-booster sending you straight into Discovery, the stage where things really start to look up. You've moved beyond anger and resistance—isn't that enough? Not really. Make room for Stage 3, *Discomfort*. It's a transitional stage, a crossroads where depending on how things go you either develop momentum carrying you toward the green stages or you run into issues akin to your car stalling, grinding gears, even slipping into reverse.

The rub is this: having made whatever peace you have made with the change, having taken some ownership, now you have to deal with it. It's here, it's happening, you're no longer fighting or denying. You are starting to carry out your role in the implementation or upgrade or evolution and it's not easy. Reality has arrived. It's sinking in.

And so some of us sink a little. The change can feel like a weight. In Stage 3, with the energy of anger gone, we start experiencing other things, not all of them conducive to productivity and workplace happiness. Things like indecision and absentmindedness. Lethargy. Even a feeling of being overwhelmed. At its worst, here, the weight of the accepted and now-being-implemented change can push some people toward dysphoria and despair.

Dysphoria, for those scoring at home, comes from a Greek phrase meaning "hard to bear." A fancy word for being in a state of unhappiness. Non-euphoria.

Think of your change as a jigsaw puzzle. In Stage 1, you're greeted with a scatter of colored shapes on a table, and you don't even have the puzzle-box with the image for guidance. It can feel hopeless. In Stage 2, you go looking for the box. You find it. In Stage 3, you return to the table holding the box, and not only is that jumble of pieces daunting in its chaos but the image on the box is complex: multiple tiny figures, subtle color gradations.

But at least now you have the picture.

Breaking Through, Not Breaking Down

Stage 3 can be a stage of sighs. Sure, you're no longer tempted to sweep your arm across the card table and send the puzzle pieces flying, but staring at that jumble, you realize with a jolt that you've really got your work cut out for you. *Where do I start?* you think. *I could be here all night.*

Managers, leaders, your Stage 3 challenge is less about communicating, clarifying, and getting people to buy in than it is about helping employees avoid feeling buried under the new tasks, procedures, roles, products. Roll out the newness incrementally, in doable chunks, and have ready ways to keep people's energy up. No matter how alert to signs of sluggishness and information overload you are—and no matter how creative when it comes to energizing your workforce—it will still pay to plan for some slowdown during Stage 3. Workers tend to feel less than 100%. Absenteeism will increase. And be aware, too, of burying yourself.

Employees, experiencing malaise at this middle point in your change journey is both normal and common. We've seen it happen time and again. You work to get your arms around the change, and now you have to carry what you hold, finish line a ways off.

But by knowing what to expect in Stage 3, both those going through it and those in a supervisory capacity can be prepared and vigilant. Better yet, this chapter shows people how to minimize their stay in Stage 3 Discomfort. And to those who are there now, take heart: what follows is a much more comfortable stage, *Discovery*. Soon the wind will be at your back.

How We Feel in Stage 3: Anxious

On one level, we're feeling some relief. Some of those Stage 1 fears and worries turned out to be exaggerated or even groundless. That across-the-board negativity that hit some of us on hearing the change announcement has lightened. Not being angry all day feels okay, too.

Still, we may come to work feeling uncertain, a little wary, not quite ourselves. We might be tired. Or at least more tired than normal. Why? You're assimilating. You're organizing and categorizing the newness so you can regain that pre-change sense of control. And so you can do your job better. But uncertainty lingers—there's a lot to take in. You might even wonder if you're up to it. Maybe you're working with a person who seems to have it all figured out and who shows up every day in a super-chipper state, decked out in company logo-wear. You might roll your eyes, but you also have a moment where you feel a little "slow" or "inept" or "out of it." Don't be too hard on yourself. People learn at different speeds, and that's what's going on: you're learning. Your brain is busily categorizing, processing—creating new pathways for the new experiences and knowledge. Besides, logo-wear never solved anything. Nor can we rule out the possibility that Mr. or Ms. Perky might be putting up a front.

How We Think in Stage 3: Confused

A great thinker once said, "Confusion is the final step before learning." Which is all well and good, but the problem with confusion is it drags down your confidence and with it your energy. Listlessness might spread from work to home. And confidence issues are typical in

Stage 3. The *Why this?* and *Why me?* and *Why now?* questions of the first two stages have given way to *What now?* and *What next?* and *How do they expect me to do all of this?* Even in a passage through only mild Stage 3 discomfort, attitudes can drift toward pessimism and defeatism. Problems, problems—everything looks like a problem.

How We Act in Stage 3: Unproductive

Feeling lethargic is a drag. Things are piling up and you're getting farther and farther behind, at work and at home. You say you "don't care" now, but you know what that will mean later. You still don't care? Well, you will, eventually.

Being unproductive increases the levels of anxiety and confusion, creating a daily circle of frustration. Easily distracted, you may have difficulty with even everyday tasks. And your inability to get anything significant completed is doing a number on your self-esteem.

An employee shared this Stage 3 moment in one of our training sessions:

> I knew I had overslept. The hotel wake-up call hadn't come. I started crying. Outside it was raining, and the thought of walking the three blocks to my client's office in the blustery cold only made me feel worse. I was tired. Burnt-out. Ready to quit. Overwhelmed. I pulled the covers over my head and tried to find the energy to face the day. That's when I really woke up and realized it was Saturday—I was

home, lying in my own bed. I had been dreaming of
my business trip to Boston earlier in the week.

To Know More, Notice More

Even highly organized, normally energetic people can
sink into the slough of Stage 3. You're clearer on the
change but waiting for motivation. Here are some of the
signs:

▽ Becomes frustrated, even overwhelmed at times

▽ Worried about the future

▽ Easily distracted

▽ Difficulty managing medium- and long-term tasks

▽ Dismal outlook on things

▽ Sluggishness

▽ Inconsistent workplace attitude

▽ Lower quality work

▽ Unable to prioritize

Language from people struggling in Stage 3:

▽ "I'm not sure what I should do first."

▽ "I just don't care."

▽ "I believe I am just working hard for nothing."

▽ "There's no way I'm going to finish this."

▽ "I'm overwhelmed and tired all the time."

▽ "I feel really nervous about my future here."

A Powered-Down World

Managers, it helps to have a stage-appropriate sense of what people are capable of delivering work-wise inside the energy-challenged world of Stage 3. Here are things you should consider *not* doing while implementing change during Stage 3:

▽ **Allowing people to work a lot of extra hours**
Working more does not normally produce better quality or greater results in this stage. In fact, it can slow down progress and add to employees' sense of being overwhelmed.

▽ **Assuming that productivity will remain the same**
It won't. Prepare and plan for a slowdown time. You can goose levels of productivity by setting clear priorities and keeping employees focused on specific tasks.

▽ **Assigning big, new projects**
In Stage 3, employee lethargy and confusion around priorities is high, and energy and motivation low. Direct employee focus only toward necessary tasks.

▽ **Staying away from your work unit**
This is a time when people need support. A manager's unavailability can reinforce frustration. Being available and encouraging will limit the slowdown.

Employees, you can do yourself a Stage 3 favor by taking the following actions:

▽ Focusing on short-term tasks

▽ Realizing that difficulty prioritizing and a lack of detail clarity is normal in Stage 3

▽ Being realistic about what performance results to expect right now

▽ Finding ways to beat frustration with creative distractions and motivation

Case in Point: Naybor Co.

After the merger, the data-processing group at Naybor Co. had plenty to repair—faulty systems on the tech side and broken confidences on the human side. The staff was exhausted, burned out. After weeks of working long hours with multiple challenges, morale was low.

Erin was a team leader in the data transfer group. Her exceptional organizational skills and friendly personality make her both easy to work with and someone who consistently gets the job done right and on time. Lately, however, she has been impatient with nearly everyone and unusually quiet at staff meetings. This has had a ripple effect on other team members. Because when Erin is good, everything is good. When Erin is bad . . .

> I have been so disappointed with the way this merger has been handled that it has taken the wind out of my sails. Several people in my group are being RIF'ed and they don't know it yet. I feel bad not being able to tell them the truth about their work future. I feel torn between my loyalty to the

company and my responsibility to my staff. I am really frustrated and struggling to keep up a good front. This distraction has affected the quality of my work. I can't seem to stay focused.

David was a process planner for the system implementation the merger entailed. He had done a great job communicating how things would be handled and preparing the staff for new information and reporting requirements. Everything seemed well-designed, ready to go. But when it came time to actually implement the changes, problems arrived and things ground to a halt—including David. He called in sick three days in a row. From here things just got worse.

The delays due to the equipment failures over-whelmed me. I couldn't get anyone to authorize funds for the repairs and replacement parts we needed. The implementation was a complex under-taking. There was little room for error and manage-ment had so overpromised on our capability to make this all happen on a shoestring budget and tight schedule that I could hardly bear the stress. I haven't seen much of my family for weeks since I'm always here, seemingly spinning my wheels.

Both Erin and David went into their change techni-cally well-prepared, eyes wide open. Yet both were buffeted by the reality of how the merger actually unfolded. In classic Stage 3 fashion, their confidence took a hit, their mental sharpness declined, their productivity suffered. What they weren't prepared for was how they themselves would react as the change hit roadblocks. They did everything they could in terms of externals—but the internal tripped them up.

Stage Priority: Finding Motivation

> Both tears and sweat are salty, but they render a
> different result. Tears will get you sympathy;
> sweat will get you change.
>
> *J. Jackson*

If you think of your change journey as a passage from night to day—darkness to light—then Stage 3 is daybreak. You're starting to pick out objects in the early light, just as your sleepy mind and body are starting to take on the clarity and energy you'll need for the day. Limbo's probably not the right word but Stage 3 is something of an in-between phase, with all the push-pull, bitter-sweet, and up-and-down that that implies. A horizon stage. Are you going to rise and meet the day, or are you going to hit snooze, fall back on the pillow, and pull the blanket over your head?

You may feel like doing the latter but resist the urge. Self-motivation is never more important than in Stage 3. Good management can help, obviously, but in the end, with the change going forward, final motivation must come from within. You know yourself best: one person's rejuvenating distraction is another person's form of procrastination. Extend your self-knowledge to the gremlins of Stage 3: lethargy, feeling scattered, frustration. What energizes you? What helps you regain focus? What has worked in the past to reduce frustration?

Erin and David may very well have gotten through Stages 1 and 2 with little trouble, but they had not planned for the trials of Stage 3 and were caught off guard when they suddenly felt overwhelmed and less than fully competent at their jobs. Had they known they'd entered Stage 3 in The Change Cycle, and used the self-awareness tools presented in this book, they might have reacted more effectively. Instead, they withdrew: Erin emotionally, David literally.

These questions are designed to help you think more about what specifically motivates you and what tends to work as an internal obstacle, energy drain, or confidence thief:

▽ Do I self-motivate or need a boss, spouse, or deadline to get me moving?

▽ Am I motivated most by achievement? Duty? Fear of punishment? Need for safety?

▽ When I'm frustrated, do I keep banging away, redirect, goof around, or quit?

▽ Do I ever sabotage myself from doing what I know would be helpful or beneficial?

▽ How long do I play that game before taking the next needed step?

▽ When I delay, is it because I'm feeling incapable, lackadaisical, angry, or exhausted?

▽ What tends to be the trigger when I finally step into action?

▽ How much do I rely on others? The right amount? Too little? Too much?

▽ What advice would I give someone in a situation similar to mine?

▽ Who could best help me with my biggest work issue right now?

▽ Have I been "self-medicating"? (Drinking? Drugs? Food?)

▽ Have I been feeling unusually sad? Hopeless? Completely wiped out?

▽ If I said yes to one or both of the last two questions, should I seek professional help?

Depression and substance abuse—though not frequent consequences of workplace change—are not unheard-of either. And when depression occurs in Stage 3, it can sometimes arrive more stealthily than in Stage 1, when it's often easier to establish a cause-and-effect link between the change announcement and a sudden mood decline. So be alert to changes in your affect, outlook, and energy levels at this midpoint in the cycle. Managers, you too will want to watch for signs of deteriorating attitude and unhealthy behavior in your employees.

The Value of Reframing

Rather than needing professional help, most of us can address Stage 3 discomfort ourselves, using self-assessment, reframing, and other cognitive tools. And of course even those suffering serious mood disorders are frequently taught to use the same tools, whether or not medication is also involved. "Cognitive therapy"—a therapy that teaches people to recognize self-defeating thought patterns and how to access more empowering thoughts—continues to yield impressive results. Similarly, in reframing we examine the ways we look at and internally "talk" about a problem and find ways to reframe things in a more positive light. The challenges to spirit, body, and schedule as a workplace change rolls out in Stage 3 can darken our general outlook. You're tired, you're frustrated—we all know how this affects our perception of things.

It's not that you want to activate some kind of Inner Pollyanna, rose-coloring the world. You don't have to turn into Mr. or Ms. Perky. It's just that at this point in The Change Cycle, there might be some gloom on your lens. Is it fully warranted? Below is some more common Stage 3 language people use, both aloud and to themselves. Often with a sigh. If your internal dialogue sounds like this a lot of the time, not only is it unlikely to be helping but it may end up keeping you stuck in Stage 3 Discomfort longer than necessary.

▽ "No matter how much I work, they expect more."

▽ "This is useless."

▽ "Whatever . . ."

▽ "I can't catch up on all I have to do."

▽ "I'm never this disorganized."

▽ "I feel like I'm beating my head against the wall."

▽ "Do they have any idea how hard this is?"

Talk that moves you forward:

▽ "I'm more than halfway done."

▽ "Time to focus on stuff I can actually control."

▽ "Would I really want management to expect less of me?"

▽ "Telling myself I can't catch up won't help me catch up."

▽ "I've gotten through every big change before."

▽ "Even a thousand-mile trek begins with a single step."

▽ "In the past, it usually helped when I asked for help."

▽ "Nothing ventured, nothing gained."

Note the reframing going on above. Things like fatigue, management expectations, and the complexity of new tasks are no longer occasions for dispirited sighs but instead are reframed in ways that can provide encouragement and motivation. The self-talk above is solution-centered. It's realistic. It's nonblaming. It contains perspective. It looks back, but it looks back at what worked, rather than dwelling on past frustrations or failures.

Psychologists have found that depressed people, in looking back, obsess about what didn't go well or work out. They almost literally seem to forget past successes. Part of their therapy is learning how to access positive memories and use them to ward off negative ones.

Conversely, reframing is a central trait of successful people. In fact, some of the highest achievers have an almost overactive reframing muscle. Not only do they barely seem to remember things that didn't work out, if presented with an example of what most of us would consider a nonsuccess in their past, they are quickly able to find positives. *Me fail? No way!*

Let's assume being an overactive reframer is not something you have to worry about at the moment. Most of us could do with improving our reframing skills.

Here's more reframing in action. The new "picture" is in italics:

▽ "I feel totally overwhelmed. There aren't enough hours in the day."
This is one serious workload. Time to prioritize, make a to-do list.

▽ "Everyone around me is already up to speed."
It's not how fast I catch on, it's how well I learn.

▽ "This schedule is nuts. I'm gonna get sick."
Last time work got like this, eating better and exercising helped.

▽ "This change is ridiculous!"
Hopefully the change will make sense soon.

Learning Curves

Accurate self-appraisal when it comes to your own workplace effort and attitude is not an easy or elementary thing, but it can be improved with honest, conscious attention. You've probably worked with people whose self-measurements seem a little off. They might be working less hard and less productively than anyone else in the unit and yet often they're the first person to declare, *I need to cut myself some slack!* or *Man,*

I need a vacation! Or even, *You know how they say work smarter, not harder? I need to try and put that into practice!*

Let's say you're not that person. The majority of us are susceptible to something else. When frustrated by Stage 3 gremlins (falling behind, losing focus, feeling tired), we sometimes feel if we just keep pounding away, fatigue be damned (and maybe meals, exercise, and family ignored, too), eventually we'll get it, get caught up, get that desk clear or quota filled. Maybe. But ask yourself: At what point are you working your own rock-pile variation on that famous definition of, well, insanity? *Doing the same thing over and over and expecting a different result.*

In other words, when does persistence become . . . unhelpful compulsion?

The history of achievement is full of stories of people whose work or creative breakthroughs did not happen "on the job" but while doing something else. You could probably write a whole book about people who had their lightbulb moment while doing something mundane—like the laundry.

Distraction. Here it's neither a bad word, nor a bad thing. It might be exactly what you need. Once again clear-eyed self-assessment comes in handy. You know yourself best. It's up to you to survey your work and achievement record and establish guidelines for delineating between a productive distraction and counterproductive things like procrastination, diminishing the size of the task, running from the problem, sticking head in sand.

Sometimes even little things can help you get unstuck (and thus prove not so little):

▽ Driving a new way to work

▽ Taking the stairs instead of the elevator

▽ Adding a new work-out or extra miles to your exercise

▽ Trying a new restaurant

▽ Catching a new movie

▽ Starting that book that's been on your night table for three months

▽ Getting up to watch the sunrise

▽ Discovering some new music

▽ Test-driving a sports car

▽ Going to a zoo (or aquarium) for the first time in years

The list goes on. No doubt you could come up with another dozen yourself. What you want to do is break free of the familiar. The mind needs this right now—and it thanks you.

A Word on Behalf of Sleep

Another temptation in Stage 3 is to devote less time to sleep and more to conquering the workplace change. Needless to say, if you're on some kind of deadline and you have no choice—well, you have no choice. But keep in mind, research continues to underline the importance of sleep in human functioning, not least when it comes to learning and mastering new skills. The day's learning is not finalized—does not fully come together—until a night of good sleep is logged. The research word for this coming together, this deep learning, is *consolidation*. So rather than pushing harder, think about getting an extra hour of sleep one of these Stage 3 nights. (Added bonus: supposedly sleep helps you lose weight!)

Case in Point: Monztero Inc.

As the deadline for the new implementation neared, Fran's stress level was higher than a thermometer in the hot July sun. Manager of financial services, she had a critical stake in having the system change come off smoothly. Things had been tense through several weeks of preparation, and the work remaining was complex to the point of seeming overwhelming.

Fran's management skills had been stretched to the breaking point, and that mixed with disappointment in some colleagues and frustration with the boss made for tough times at the office. If quitting was a real option, she'd be tempted to walk out the door right now.

Luckily for all involved, she adopted a one-day-at-a-time attitude and persevered.

> I tried to be as clear and concise as I could in terms of what was needed in order to manage—and at times lead—my department through the implementation. I drafted a specific set of objectives for each work group and assisted them in planning their step-by-step approach to task completion. I also decided to share with my staff my frustrations with the project, but followed that up with my sincere belief that it would

all eventually be worth the struggle. And I put into literal practice that maxim "When life gives you lemons, make lemonade." I added it as the signature of my emails, and every Monday morning I brought three gallons of lemonade for the coffee station. Slowly but surely my normally positive outlook on things started to return. And along with it, my sense of humor.

Learning Curves

To pass beyond the discomfort of Stage 3, find ways to brighten your attitude both at work and outside work. Creative distractions are in order, as is the accomplishment of doable tasks. Actions—rather than thinking, which in Stage 3 can quickly become over-thinking and brooding—often help. Movement through space, physical exercise. Motion by the body can move things in the mind. Work-wise, don't try to fix it all at once. Start small. Work with what you know. Once we are in motion and feeling semi-productive again, we find ourselves, like Jessica, with a determination to "see it through." She acted her way into right thinking.

Stage 3 things to welcome and avoid signal the importance of doing, of finding energy.

Things to Avoid in Stage 3

▽ **Asking too much of yourself**

Help yourself by focusing on small chunks of work and setting short-term deadlines. How do you eat an elephant? One bite at a time.

▽ **Grinding**

Be conscious of crossing that line dividing admirable stick-to-it-ive-ness from . . . diminishing returns.

▽ **Throwing in the towel**

Expect frustration. Expect some confusion. But things will get better. So don't use how you're feeling and working now as the basis to judge a project's worthiness.

Things to Welcome in Stage 3

▽ **Task realism**

Plan for things to take longer than they should. Keep your stress from escalating—if something should take two hours, plan for three. Under-promise, over-deliver.

▽ **Diversions**

To get your energy and focus back, consider a healthy diversion (or three).

▽ **The Five P's**

Patience, Perspective, Persistence, Play, Purpose. Practice them.

Patience: It takes time to assimilate change. And don't forget it was the tortoise who won the race.

Perspective: The change fog has lifted. No scenic overlook yet, but at least there's a view down the road.

Persistence: Strive for a level of activity that keeps you focused and moving, not bleary and robotic.

Play: What gives you a boost? Lightens your mood? Now's a good time for this.

Purpose: Remind yourself that all this work transports you toward your goal: thriving post-change.

Keys to Moving On

▽ Engage motivation.

▽ Accomplish enough to stay in motion.

▽ Ask, "What steps can I take to expedite a break-through?"

Remember "Don't Just Do Something, Sit There" from Stage 2? Here—and it's a sign you've made progress—you're ready to reverse that slogan: *Don't Just Sit There, Do Something!* In the red stages, you needed to gather more information and start processing it. As with a person in a dark room, sudden movement was not recommended. In Stage 1 you could bump into something and fall. In Stage 2 there was a risk of rashness, even lashing out. Here, moving out of Stage 3, you have better vision, and there is light. You're not acting out of fear or anger—you're acting on behalf of the change, with growing focus, looking forward.

If you don't feel quite "right" yet, remind yourself that you've already traveled a distance. Even if you're not yet running on all cylinders, there is some serious road at your back. And with what you've picked up from these pages, you're ahead of the game anyway. So take a step. And then another. Chances are, the headwind's gone. Finally.

Note to Self:

The answer is going with the wind.
Now would be good.

The Danger Zone

Most of us do move forward—and step into Discovery. On occasion, however, people get stuck in Stage 3, their condition of discomfort so strong, or perhaps simply lasting so long, that dejected doors open and Fear & Friends step back in. Sometimes the quicksand is an unexpected event or sudden disappointment linked to the change: your unit's project loses funding, your promotion doesn't happen. Other times it may not be personal to you, beyond the fact that you're part of the team undergoing the change. Management, disheartened by the plodding pace or by multiple snags, loses patience and openly considers scrapping the change to regain control—or worse, actually does scrap the change.

Result? A bunch of employees in discomfort are now sent all the way back to Stage 1.

The Danger Zone is akin to backsliding, falling off the wagon. Signs to watch for in yourself are a steady urge to give up, a feeling of being useless, a belief that nothing's working out. Just as management's patience is needed in any workplace change, so you need to be patient with yourself if getting back your pre-change stride seems to be taking too long. But if fear and anger start cropping up again and clouding your mind, remember you have acquired some tools to help take them on. Revisit lessons shared in chapters one and two of this book. With luck you will get yourself out of red-stage perspectives and keep moving all the way through Stage 3 this time. Once you hit Discovery, there's no looking back.

Chapter Four

Decide, Then Take Your Best Step

The real voyage of discovery consists not in seeking new
landscapes, but in having new eyes.

Marcel Proust

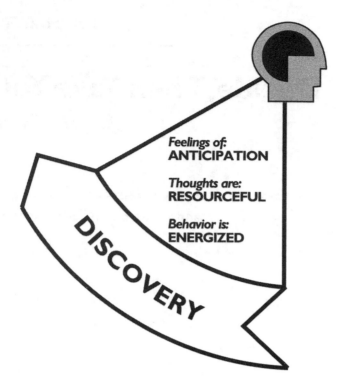

Stage 4: Trekking from Discovery to Perspective

It's not quite yellow-jersey time, but if you've made it to Stage 4, *Discovery*, you're getting close. Some good news right off the bat: entering this energetic, hopeful stage makes it almost a lock you'll go on and reach the end of The Change Cycle. Furthermore, there's no more fighting and slogging as you work toward completion, only some choice-points and manageable challenges that engage your powers of self-reliance and resolve.

Managers and leaders, take note: since employee autonomy thrives here, your role becomes more one of a supportive facilitator than a directive task manager. Employees, take heart in knowing you'll have less need to look outside yourself for information and guidance. That said, the Discovery stage is not just about flying solo. It's also very much about working together. And not in some dreary forced-cooperation way, or a team-building exercise in the parking lot. You don't have to *take one for the team*. No, what makes this a collaborative stretch in The Change Cycle is that you and those you work with are primed for real interactivity, a sharing of ideas and methods, without anxiety or defensiveness.

It's a synergy stage. People are pulling in the same direction.

Are you home free? Well, we did mention challenges. And Discovery is colored yellow, not green. There are some who do get stalled here. But those who stall usually restart, and the vast majority of us who reach Stage 4 never look back.

This chapter helps you find your way in the Discovery stage, and then move beyond it.

"I, Resource"

Remember the Will Smith futuristic thriller *I, Robot*? It's a catchy title (from an Isaac Asimov sci-fi story of the same name), so credit where credit's due for the name of this section heading: "I, Resource." Just ignore any associations with a robot uprising.

Of course all along we've been encouraging you to be self-resourceful, emphasizing the value of inward assessing, monitoring, listening, and so forth, as you move through the first three stages. But we have also advocated outreach to others, because until now getting unstuck often meant answering questions such as *Who could best help me with my biggest work issue right now?* But things are different now. The tools and resources you need to keep moving are well within your grasp. You've done the prep; you're fully equipped. It's mainly a matter of reaching within. (A cheer just went up from the "wing-tips" of the world.)

The road you're on is beginning to slope downhill. There are new things to see (new things to discover) along the way, and there are some curves and a few forks, but gravity is your friend now. Along with your decision-making ability and penchant for finding solutions.

You're up to speed data-wise. Your sense of control is returning, and with it, energy. The key is to capitalize. In Stage 3 you were seeking ways both at work and at home to put more gas in your tank; here you're fueled up and your mission is to take advantage. Stage-recognition helps. Is there more bounce in your step? Are you concentrating better? You don't have to say it aloud but go ahead and think it: *Hey, I'm in the Discovery stage!*

Having thought the thought, it's time to walk the walk. You're ready to meet job challenges brought about by the change. You're ready for new projects, ready to dive in. Utilize that energy. Consider ways to boost it even further. To paraphrase a line from that old TV show *The*

Six Million Dollar Man: "You have the technology." Your "on" switch is flipped.

I, Resource.

How We Feel in Stage 4: Anticipatory

Anticipation is the name of the emotional game in Stage 4. Yes, finally an A-word expressing something we'd actually like to experience (as opposed to Anxiety, Angst, Alarm, Alienation, and AGH!). You still may not applaud the change (and may never), but you've come far enough to feel some hope when you consider the newness the change is bringing—new rhythms, exchanges, possibilities. Having made some peace with the change and realized you can hack it, you're also starting to think things might actually turn out okay and the thought stirs a little excitement.

There are no guarantees, but you want to see what happens.

Some people tell us they think this may be the first time they've reached the Discovery stage when it comes to a change at work. Possibly, but more likely their negative view of change (change equals disruption, frustration, struggle, the unknown) framed past experiences in a way that had them remembering only the rough early stages. If change means misery, that's all you see or remember.

Understanding the full process makes change less scary and provides "stage-awareness," allowing you to calibrate your reactions and make the most of your present cycle location.

Where the first three stages were about impact, survival, and security, the fourth stage is about energy, openness, and opportunities. Entitlement issues and *What about me?* questions give way to *I can* and *Let's try it* and a resourceful "What if?" attitude. Anything to watch out for? Well, anticipation is one thing, giddiness another. Some people's (over)enthusiasm can mask an uncertainty about what actually to do next, a kind of variation on nervous laughter. Another trap is when enthusiasm triggers over-preparation, driving a person to know "everything" related to the issue so as to make the "perfect" decision every step of the way. Feeling anticipation, even excitement? Welcome it. Just run a quick check of its solidity and its effect on your performance.

How We Think in Stage 4: Resourcefully

Discovery brings *perspective*. Where early stages induced a kind of tunnel-vision, with focus tending to be small and obsessive, here your view broadens and with it comes a receptivity to new choices and the ideas of others. No longer does everything look like a problem, an obstacle, a landmine, a detour. Your expanded outlook allows for what one influential expert in management theory calls "Appreciative Inquiry." AI, as it is sometimes called, is a way of assessing workplace challenges that focuses not on deficits and needs, but rather on possibilities and capabilities. In contrast to a "troubleshooting" or "problem-tackling" mindset, here a more affirmative orientation works to build on strengths and to deepen appreciation for assets.

And the result? Proponents point to increased energy, greater resourcefulness, and higher productivity, at both the employee and organizational levels. People's sense of their potential rises. They feel a greater sense of curiosity. They feel mobilized. Interestingly, the AI approach asks employees to remember "peak experiences," those times in life when they felt most capable and energetic. With positive memories retrieved, people are able to act as their own coach, inspiring themselves to dream bigger and to strive for a higher level of achievement. Not unlike The Change Cycle approach with its emphasis on "reframing" and making memory work for, not against, you, AI recognizes that we have a measure of control over what we highlight from the past and what we "see" in the present.

We're not simply at the mercy of what has been and what is. We have the power of interpretation. Appreciative Inquiry asks, *Do you choose to see constraints and roadblocks, or opportunities for growth and break-throughs?* Successful people tend to see possibilities, not hurdles. And they find ways to cultivate this vision, as consciously and robustly as they can.

In the Discovery stage, your work inquiries—your explorations of what needs to be done, and how to accomplish what needs to be done—take on a more appreciative, a more affirmative, cast. You recognize your strengths and begin to play from them. You see strengths around you. You start discovering things. Ride this positivity. Entertain your ideas, follow your thoughts, explore your options. And do the same for the ideas of others, the inspirations of fellow discoverers.

How We Act in Stage 4: Energized

We get more done. We've regained the juice. It helps that we are now working with the change, rather than fighting against it. It's easier to get up in the morning, easier to leave for work. You can put in a long day and still have something left.

You're also finding it easier to partner with co-workers, to work jointly on solutions.

The draining forces of doubt, anger, discomfort—you don't miss them.

Can anything block this increased action and collaboration? Yes, and it's a version of analysis paralysis. Some people suddenly see so many options, feel confronted with so many decisions in need of making, that they can't push the start button.

To Know More, Notice More

People moving through the Discovery stage:

▽ Offer new ideas

▽ Feel energized

▽ Eagerly work with others toward a common solution or goal

▽ Demonstrate insight into ways to move forward

▽ Explore options and choices

▽ Create a sense of teamwork

▽ Motivate and energize others

▽ Readily plan short-term and long-term goals

Someone stalling in Stage 4:

▽ Feels moody and tired

▽ Obsessively prepares

▽ Asks endless questions

▽ Tinkers and tinkers at some small task

▽ Exhibits gung-ho attitude, but little follow-through

▽ Praises change but is slow to implement

▽ Can't make a decision

Language from people moving through Discovery:

▽ "I'm seeing more options than I did before."

▽ "I'm determined to reorder my priorities."

▽ "It's up to me to choose."

▽ "It seems like almost overnight I felt better."

▽ "I feel like I have the tools to make this work."

▽ "I'm starting to understand other viewpoints."

Language from people stalling:

▽ "I know what I need to do, I just can't pull the trigger."

▽ "I can't do anything else until I get this first part exactly right."

▽ "There may be a better idea out there so we'd better wait a bit."

▽ "I know it seems like I've already asked this, but . . ."

▽ "Is there any way we could get to that later?"

▽ "I don't understand how you can see it that way."

Managers, here are things to steer clear of when supervising those in Stage 4:

▽ **The buffet mentality**
Being overly accommodating—offering too many options—while seeking employee buy-in can actually work against you. *Something for everyone* sometimes overcomplicates decision-making. It can leave employees vulnerable to second-guessing their choice and comparing their deal to others. Keeping things simple is often the better approach. People tend to adapt more quickly than they customize.

▽ **Micro-management**
Allow for more worker autonomy in this stage. They're ready for it. They have the skills, perspective, drive. Coach yourself to back away and let people draw on their own ideas and strengths. When you step in, offer encouragement and affirmation.

▽ **Judging ideas after inviting people to brainstorm**
Fostering input is good, but proceeding to openly grade ideas not so good. People will be slow to offer suggestions and solutions if they think what they say is on public trial.

▽ **Being seen as someone threatened by other people's promising ideas**
It doesn't take much to convince employees that management likes to take credit for every good idea. Be careful of supporting this viewpoint. Trust quickly erodes and workers clam up.

Stage 4 Priority: Make Decisions Using Expanded Perspective

With your increased capacity for taking in alternative perspectives and looking at issues from different angles comes the challenge of using this broadened vision to identify the best options among the many you now survey and to choose one. You have a solid information foundation to work from. You can entertain a broad range of ideas and advice from different people without losing clarity of vision. What's more, you've regained your faith that by tapping into your own instincts and experience you can guide yourself forward. So your Stage 4 mission is to make the right decisions, take the right action.

Case in Point: Talstone Inc.

Winning the contract to manufacture the new MBN product line was a much-needed victory for everyone at Talstone Inc. After years of planning and untold hours of dedicated, detailed work, the future held exciting new possibilities. Differences in perspective between management and operations had led to frequently strained communication, but in the end the synergy of their convictions and a merging of data and ideas created the winning bid.

People were surprised when it was announced Cesar would lead the Specs and Docs team. In fact, the announcement took away some of the excitement people were feeling for the project. Though he had plenty of tech know-how, Cesar had never been much of a team player, and this project group needed to bridge knowledge gaps between two very different operations functions. A skilled manager and communicator would be needed to create a sufficiently "we" attitude and approach to this complex job.

Early on, however, when the team needed precise direction and instruction, Cesar delivered. He was all about getting the right people in the right places with the tools they needed, while keeping an eye on the clock. But as things came together and the team reached the Discovery stage, Cesar's micro-managing style became less affective. A more collaborative approach was necessary. Team members started wondering about Cesar's leadership suitability.

Cesar himself was starting to have questions. As he recalls:

> Getting the MBN contract was one of the highlights of my career. Never had I worked with such a dedicated group of folks. We had our struggles at times, but because they trusted me, I kept us afloat through the tough start-up period. Then we hit the next phase of the project, a crossroads. My attention to detail, a management asset and strength in the beginning, was no longer proving to be such a positive.
>
> It was a tough decision, but I resigned as project leader. I didn't ask off the team, though, as I wanted to do all I could to make sure what we'd accomplished to that point didn't go down the drain. My boss Mike was pretty surprised when I told him my decision. He thanked me for my loyalty and asked who I thought would be a good replacement. I encouraged him to appoint Jackie because she had

both a good knowledge-base and strong people and communication skills. He said he'd consider it.

That afternoon, Mike called us all together and told the team what I had done. I was genuinely surprised at the nice things people said. Mike then surprised us by asking the team for input as to who should be the new team leader. After some frank and candid comments about where we were on task and what needed to be accomplished, the group decided the best option would be to have Jackie and I co-lead. Jackie confidently and immediately said, "Yes." And I, to my own surprise, answered, "Definitely!"

Here we see a group of employees in the Discovery stage. Note the hallmarks: openness, dialogue, confidence, flexibility, teamwork. And a lucid, nondefensive assessment of capabilities. The thinking is both solution-based and "outside the box." Result? A creative resolution: a co-leadership position. These people are moving on. The green stages beckon.

By contrast, consider this story from the same company transition. For nearly a year Sandy had been looking for property for the new distribution center Talstone would build if it won the MBN contract. Monies had been allocated. When a prime parcel became available, the plan was Talstone would buy it. The new distribution facility was one of the foundations of the project. If they didn't get the contract, the land would be sold. They got the contract and the project began immediately. But there was no real estate to begin construction on.

As Sandy tells it:

At first there were so many properties to choose from within our specs that I took a careful wait-and-see attitude. I wanted to make sure we got the absolute best plot of land. I held back on a few prime pieces, and eventually we lost them in bidding wars. Almost before I realized what happened, the choices thinned out. Then prices started rising dramatically, and management put pressure on me to make a purchase fast.

My boss became impatient and said she wanted the property and all necessary permits in hand "yesterday." I checked into a few more parcels that didn't exactly meet our specifications, but seemed to have merit. Another week went by as I weighed our options, and I had several potentially good possibilities lined up. But before I could decide on one and put the purchase through, my boss informed me I'd been reassigned.

Learning Curves

Sandy's story illustrates a Stage 4 trap. You have the know-how, you're back in the driver's seat, your priority project defines your role in the change, and just when you need it, decisiveness drains away. It's one thing to know what needs to be done, another to do it.

That's the rub. Yes, you've progressed beyond the chaos and powerlessness of those early stages, when you felt vulnerable to decisions dropped from on high. But now that you have some power to decide, you need to decide. For some people, a Hamlet problem arises—A

Crisis of Decisiveness. In Shakespeare's famous tragedy, Hamlet can't decide on a course of action. He waffles on avenging his father's murder and even on whether to live ("to be") or not.

And so he's become synonymous with The Man Who Couldn't Make Up His Mind.

In Sandy's case, her track record when it came to decisiveness had probably been a good one up until this point—if it hadn't, she wouldn't have been given the assignment to buy the critical parcel. But sometimes a change can do this to us. We think the challenges are finally behind us, we're ready to play our part in carrying the company forward, we may even be bullish on the future. But wait. Something has sneaked up on us. Suddenly we can't close, can't decide.

This compulsion to make the "perfect" decision can be one cause of freezing up. The size of the change may have activated an unhelpful perfectionism in Sandy. What she needed to do was take a step back from the nuts-and-bolts of the search and reflect on her process, gain some perspective. Instead, she kept her head down and kept trying to find parcel-specs nirvana.

New research on decision-making may be relevant here. In today's world the number of options when it comes to almost everything has multiplied exponentially. Whether in consumer goods, where to live, career paths, even mate selection, we all have many choices. But as researchers emphasize, the human mind evolved in environments of sharply limited choice.

Are we having trouble adjusting? Many experts say yes. We tend to think of a multichoice environment as progress, as something desirable. But is it always? In a recent book called *The Paradox of Choice*, psychologist Barry Schwartz considers our option-rich world (207 kinds of energy bars! 873 shampoos!) and finds that having more choices doesn't always make people happier. It can actually do the reverse. It drags out the decision-making process. It makes people obsess about "the right choice." It leads to more "grass is always greener" thoughts. It's a lot easier to feel buyer's remorse these days. (Maybe Option 16 would have been better than Option 33!)

In almost every aspect of life, decision-making has become more complicated. Certain key decisions can be put off longer. And some of these and others can be undone more easily.

Psychologist Schwartz has a term for people like Sandy, people compelled to conduct exhaustive, nearly endless searches before choosing something, if indeed they do get around to choosing. He calls them "maximizers." They want perfection. He argues we'd be happier if we actively limit options in certain choice situations and teach ourselves that more often than not, "good enough" is good enough. He also says do less comparing of what you have with what others have.

With your Discovery stage energy, confidence, and receptivity, you're primed for some inspired, clear-eyed decisions—but also for springing into over-exploration, onto an option merry-go-around, going in circles. Unfortunately, no calculus exists to let people know precisely when they've passed from wise research into analysis paralysis. So once again call on your informed self-awareness, this time for use as a compass to see whether you're still making forward progress.

Of course—and not withstanding the welcome autonomy of this stage—here is where consultation can also help. Had Sandy gone to a colleague, described her search, and said, "Am I doing due diligence or overdoing it?", the answer may have brought quick perspective.

Discover Your Decision-Making Strategies

Take the plunge, say some motivational philosophies. *Be a risk-taker! No one ever accomplished anything without stepping into the unknown. C'mon, what do you have to lose?*

The maverick in all of us thrills to such words, and of course it's true great achievement often follows great risks. But isn't life a little more complex and uncertain than is suggested by these straight-ahead risk exhortations? Sad but true: not all risk is rewarded. Not all risk is wise. Doubtless you can think of an example or two of unwise risks when it comes to life choices. Professionally speaking, the goal for most of us is to be a moderate risk taker and to be an informed decision-maker, one who actually makes decisions as opposed to fence-sitting.

The more self-knowing you can be about your decision-making process, the better. It's easy to put yourself under enormous pressure to make the right choice or decision. Certainly when others in the workplace will be affected it only makes the stakes higher. If you're hesitant about making a decision, is it because of what others might think or say? Is it possible you've made not-deciding a comfort zone? Are you truly seeking further information, or is there something you'd rather not face or do? In order to deepen your insight into your own decision-making, here are some questions that get at how people make up their minds.

How Do You Decide?

When I make a decision

▽ I try to gather as much available information before choosing an option.

▽ I research to get a basic picture, then choose.

▽ I usually check out a few things, or sometimes just go with my gut.

When I make a significant life decision

▽ I try to look as far into the future as possible.

▽ I usually map out a year or two.

▽ I mostly consider how it affects me now.

When I make a work decision

▽ I think a fair amount about how it will impact my colleagues.

▽ I only consider how it affects me and what I do.

When I make decisions, I am more influenced by

▽ Trying to shape my future: *"This will help me get . . ."*

▽ Trying to redeem the past: *"Now they'll see I deserved that raise . . ."*

Generally I am motivated more by memories of

▽ Positive experiences and successes

▽ Failures and disappointments

Generally I am influenced more by

▽ The possibilities opened up by a decision (*"This is an excellent opportunity."*)

▽ The stability that follows a decision (*"This will keep trouble away."*)

When I have to make an important decision, I

▽ Like to consult other people. Sometimes more than a few.

▽ Mainly do my own back and forth, my own soul-searching.

When I make decisions, I am more influenced by

▽ People close to my heart: family, good friends

▽ People I respect or admire: a boss, mentor, clergy-person, former teacher

The above is not about right-way, wrong-way. It's not meant to tell you how to decide, but simply to trigger reflection. Should you see a clear decision-making pattern, however, you might want to consider how well your mode has served you and whether any adjusting or upgrading is in order.

Case in Point: Deibel Manufacturing

Alex was thrilled to be offered the position of Vice-President of Operations at the Biloxi site and accepted it immediately. The job was a significant promotion, and possibilities for further career advancement were solid. She was under no illusions regarding the professional and personal challenges, however. Biloxi had assorted production-quality problems that needed to be addressed from day one, and plant morale was at an all-time low. On the personal front, moving her family south and getting the kids adjusted to a new neighborhood, new schools, and everything else would take a significant amount of time and energy.

Alex entered her change eyes wide open. She had a baseline faith in her own resiliency. But still, in those early weeks it was tougher than she expected. Getting the family settled in was one giant, stressful scramble. Work was even tougher. For the first time in a long time, she was beset by nagging professional fears, doubts, and frustrations. *Did I make the right choice?* she wondered more than once. She kept waiting to feel a sense of progress. And waiting.

I was basically a total unknown to plant supervisors and managers. So gaining their trust didn't happen overnight. To get things back on track, I had to initiate some shift and protocol readjustments. I canvassed a broad range of opinion and though I could tell people appreciated my interest in their feedback, all that consultation also meant I was picking up their wariness and anxiety up-close, day after day. This at the same time that my kids were really wary and anxious about all the newness at home and school.

But consulting as many people as possible at the plant was important. In recent years they'd been through some poorly articulated and hastily implemented changes. I tried to redefine the work environment by encouraging management to be proactive in assessing and communicating frontline needs. There had been a long-running grudge match between management and employees, and between management levels. This bad blood had knocked down productivity at a plant that was full of high-quality workers.

I tried out new ways to overcome old issues. My managers and I made a point of emphasizing plant strengths, rather than using "deficit-talk." I considered multiple options in different arenas, and then made firm decisions while communicating my thought process. I learned as much as I could about plant particulars, but I tried not to get bogged down in tiny details. I still remember the feeling of turning a corner. Suddenly I had perspective on things. I could feel our decisions working out. Not every single person liked what we were doing, but overall, support was strong and I had people's respect. It's amazing how you can go from really wondering about yourself and what you're doing to one day feeling on solid ground again, and pretty soon after that looking forward to watching what comes together from everyone's ideas and efforts.

Without putting a name to the place she'd reached, Alex had moved into Discovery.

In Stage 4, resources open up. If Stage 3 was about being realistic when it comes to energy levels and workloads, here things are now powered-up and it's to time flip switches.

Emphasis goes to capitalizing on the restored and newly created potentials.

Things to Avoid in Stage 4

▽ Perfectionism

Use your new energy and drive to turn in the best work you can, but don't let your reawakened resources trick you into believing only flawless performance is acceptable. That's a ticket to frustration. "Perfect" can be the enemy of "good."

▽ Becoming an island

It's great to feel self-reliant again, a resource unto yourself, but remember that in certain contexts collaboration (two heads, not one) ensures a better result.

▽ Losing focus

A spike in energy, the ability to weigh multiple perspectives, creativity—these things are great pleasures of Discovery, unless they send you in too many directions at once.

Things to Welcome in Stage 4:

▽ **Innovation**

The time is right for people to do some "painting outside the lines." Boundary-breaking is not an automatic good, but in the exploratory mode that is Stage 4, experimentation by those up to speed can yield concept and productivity dividends.

▽ **Transparent decision-making**

The more open and illuminated your decision-making, your unit's, or your organization's, the better. Transparency in decision-making enhances trust, communication, and reflectiveness about this all-important process.

▽ **Unit cohesiveness**

People in the Discovery stage become both more autonomous and more collaborative, with new vigor and confidence driving both developments. While giving yourself or those you manage room to explore, simultaneously look to increase cooperation.

Keys to Moving On

▽ Channel your energy to innovate and partner

▽ Gain new insight into decision-making

▽ Ask, "What's my best next step?"

Maximizing

Maybe in your company softball league, you have what's known as a "mercy rule." They have it in Little League, too. Score ten runs in an inning and you charitably let the other team get off the field and take some more at-bats. The idea is to keep the game at least minimally competitive. And fun. Or as fun as what's shaping up to be a lopsided contest can be.

But business isn't recreational softball. You don't have to put a cap on productivity, on employee energy levels, on teamwork. Nor is "maximer" a worrisome word when applied to a company or unit—or to you—if it means making the most of new positives. The Discovery stage may not trigger the workplace equivalent of a ball team's "offensive explosion," but there's still an upsurge in the things that make a company hum: employee optimism, dynamism, and unity. So take advantage. If you're a manager or leader, harness that spirit of partnership. People have a tendency to rise to the occasion, exceeding what they might achieve working solo. Facilitate ways for employees to brainstorm and exchange ideas. Will everyone be at the same point in The Change Cycle? No. But when people join forces, they tend to interact from Discovery-stage perspectives, and those coming from earlier stages in the process tend to catch up more quickly.

People are ready to pull together. There's less of that holding back, less reticence. Less of that attitude Dilbert memorialized with his classic line, "Change is good, you go first."

We're willing to move forward side by side. Teams work.

And while you're leveraging that new energy, why not push it even higher? The thing about energy is, when you have some it's easier to get even more. In Stage 3 you came up with ways to fight the Discomfort blahs. What helped recharge your batteries? More exercise? Better eating? Changes in your home, commute, or lunch hour routines? Hitting a movie theater to watch a new comedy? Reading that inspirational biography a few minutes every night? Whatever worked, try some more. And then explore. Keep turbo-charging.

Ya gotta feed the monkey, says the surfer-dude character played by Jeff Bridges in the Coen Brothers comedy *The Big Lebowski*. It's not clear exactly what he's talking about (it never is), but it seems to have something to do with maintaining inspiration, doing what keeps you going. There are certainly loftier mantras than the one spoken by the shaggy, Hawaiian-shirt-wearing character who calls himself The Dude, but at least this one's easy to remember.

Ya gotta feed the monkey.

You're in a pioneering mood. Ride it. Discoveries made outside work will power you at work. And vice versa. Have a sci-fi spirit. Or a big-wave spirit. Go beyond. Remember how this chapter began? *I, Resource.*

Note to Self:

Rent *The Big Lebowski.*

Chapter Five

Making Sense of What Was and What Is

Change has a considerable psychological impact on the human mind. To the fearful, it is threatening because it means that things may get worse. To the hopeful, change is encouraging because things may get better. To the confident, it is inspiring because the challenge exists to make things better.

King Whitney Jr.

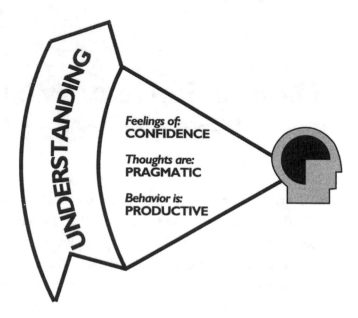

Feelings of:
CONFIDENCE

Thoughts are:
PRAGMATIC

Behavior is:
PRODUCTIVE

Stage 5: Understanding the Benefits

In work as in life, understanding sits between discovery and wisdom. You journey into newness, you map what you have seen, you move on to where you don't even need the map.

If Discovery brought an upsurge of energy, perhaps in a burst or two, and you worked to channel your renewed vigor, in Stage 5, *Understanding*, something else happens. A calmness comes. An equanimity. The change that threw your life and the life of your company or organization into a spiky, aggravating place, a place uncertain and exhausting, has now become simply a part of things, the "new normal." The rollercoaster has come to rest. Your world has leveled out.

Not that you step off the ride a zen master. Some things may still—and always—bug you. Nor would we bet you've become president of the [insert name of your change here] fan club, dispenser of buttons and souvenir mugs. No, maybe your take is closer to this person's: *I wouldn't have chosen this change and I'm pretty sure I wouldn't want to go through it again, but I will say I learned a lot along the way—about myself, about others, about change.*

How We Feel in Stage 5: Confident

Stage 5 is about self-assurance. In Discovery, you might have been charged up, even inspired, but you were still grabbing hold of things, weighing decisions, checking fuel levels. Here your touch feels sure, plus confidence—and all the good things that go with it—returns.

In Stage 5, morale is high, company-wide. People seem themselves again. Is it possible to feel good at work even though, in your heart of hearts, you still wish the change hadn't happened? Yes. It's a bit like having an annoying in-law you see once or twice a year. This person might never get any less annoying, but he or she doesn't succeed in ruining the rest of your year. (Unless you have a true "monster-in-law," a holiday Godzilla, with deep impact. In which case, our sympathies.)

It's a sign of the emotional distance you've come that one of the few Stage 5 traps is actually a case of too much self-esteem. Some people yo-yo so high from feeling low that they become impatient of those who might be a little further back in The Change Cycle. Their self-assurance hardens into an arrogance that hinders teamwork and rigidifies their thinking.

Most people, however, don't go on a Stage 5 ego trip. In fact, we often feel a little humbled, recognizing the assistance we got along the way (or maybe the push, even a kick in the rear). We realize our early-stage thinking wasn't always accurate, and we're happy for the broadening and deepening of our assessments. We feel confident—but not omnipotent.

How We Think in Stage 5: Pragmatically

Stage 5 thinking is "higher-order" thinking, to use a term from cognitive science. It's sophisticated. It's multidimensional. It excels at conceptualizing, solution-finding. The "executive brain," not the limbic region with its primitive pulses (fear! anger! envy!), is in charge.

Now is the time to take on the more mentally challenging aspects of your post-transition job. You're seeing things from multiple angles. Instead of coming at a problem with a single format of understanding, you're able to think flexibly, using a multiplicity of categories.

Lest you worry about getting over-analytic, consider this quotation. It comes from the philosopher Confucius, and it is a good way of summarizing the green-stages breakthrough:

Simplicity is the last thing learned.

The statement is less a judgment on the value of complexity vs. simplicity, and more an observation about the process of understanding. When hit with something new, when taking on a cognitive challenge, the mind tends to overcomplicate things, fueled partly by anxiety about the newness. You inevitably overthink—it's part of the process. You can't just vault to simplicity. But do the work—and it's often hard work—and your reward is clarity, a reduction of variables. Sweet simplicity.

You find the most direct, the most efficient, the most common-sense way to get it done.

How We Act in Stage 5: Productively

If energy and teamwork raised productivity in the Discovery stage, here it rises even higher as flexible thinking, job competence, consistency, and goal-setting dominate. Stage 5 is where all the initial losses in output and quality are recouped by the organization, and then some. The investment of time and money, of heart and soul, begins to pay off—for employees and management, for shareholders, vendors, customers, and communities.

People hit their strides. And the pace is steady—no more spiking up and down of energy levels, attitudes, project commitments, hours worked.

Motivation deepens. Not only that, some employees begin acting as ground-level motivators and mentors to their fellow workers. This not only helps those lagging to move forward, but also enriches mentor learning. Recent studies by education researchers have shown that learners who help their peers along gain a deep-grained knowledge of the new subject.

Managers may want to consider ways of enhancing worker-to-worker learning.

To Know More, Notice More

People moving through Stage 5:

▽ Display clear competence in post-change tasks

▽ See how ideas can be implemented

▽ Focus on the change's benefits

▽ Consistently produce

▽ Flexibly respond to continued challenges and upgrades

▽ Show appreciation for those who helped them adapt and adjust

▽ Help and mentor others

Someone stalling in Stage 5:

▽ Shows impatience with those still lagging behind

▽ Feels determined to identify every last perceived error during change

▽ Spends time closely reexamining the origin of the change

▽ Responds rigidly to ongoing readjustments

▽ Ignores the suggestions and feedback of others

Language from people in Stage 5:

▽ "I couldn't see it before, but now I understand how this can work."

▽ "A lot of people helped me through this and I really appreciate them."

▽ "I'm tired of other people being so slow to catch on."

▽ "This is working better than I thought it would."

▽ "I don't need any more feedback because I know exactly what I'm doing."

▽ "This change really did have benefits. I'm glad we did it."

▽ "We made about a million mistakes along the way."

▽ "I feel like I know enough now that I can really look ahead."

▽ "The thing is, we would have gotten to this same place anyway."

▽ "It feels great to get to this point. I say we celebrate."

Can you pick out the thrum of momentum—vs. the grinding of gears—in these statements?

Managers and leaders supervising employees in Stage 5 will want to:

▽ **Maintain focus on results**
It is important to continue affirming and empowering employees, but not at the expense of steady results. In Stage 5, you can and should expect to see results.

▽ **Refrain from being overly hands-on**
People have a clear grasp of the process by now—allow them the freedom to do their jobs and chances are they will respond. Productivity should hit new peaks here.

▽ **Mark, even celebrate progress**
If something were going wrong, you would point
it out. Do the same for what's been going right.
Doing so helps people believe in—and seek out—
success.

▽ **Prize employee confidence, not cockiness**
You want employees confident and inspired, not
brash and full of themselves.

Learning takes place in—and is vital to—all Change
Cycle stages, but most markedly here in the Understanding stage. Consider this story pointing out learning's
role in Stage 5.

Case in Point: Cadden Academy

I teach English to native Spanish speakers in a large
city. I've been doing this at the same place for twelve
years. Last year a national company bought out the
Cadden Academy. They kept all of the instructors,
but made a number of changes. The biggest was
requiring that we all use their textbook and teaching
program. It places more emphasis on writing, less on
speaking. The idea is that writing deepens thinking
overall, and so enhances learning. The writing focus
is considered a better use of classroom time because
speaking proficiency can be improved outside
class—by talking, watching movies, and so forth. The
take over was late July. I had three weeks to overhaul twelve years of road-tested curriculum.

My wife, a middle-school teacher, was sympathetic.
She'd gone through something similar with No Child

Left Behind. I know it might not sound like that big of a deal to retool a class, but that old curriculum was practically part of my DNA by this point. I could teach without notes. I knew exactly what worked and what didn't. I had total confidence, and teachers need confidence. Now I had a learning curve myself, I was entering the classroom with doubts, and I worried if my students would be getting what they needed. Most of them work one or two jobs to get by, they invest valuable time and money in our classes, and what they learn is really important for the rest of their lives.

It wasn't until October that I finally started feeling better about things. More confident. I was having fun coming up with subjects for my students to write about. I'm a jazz musician as well, and one night some students came to a club, watched me play sax, and wrote about the club and the band. We set up a website where each student posted a weekly blog. They wrote about sports, movies, food. Some of the class essays, even if the English was basic, had great details about their families, their passions, where they come from. I was learning more about my students' lives than ever.

I was also thinking more than I had in a long time about what stimulates good learning, what gets people motivated. In jazz you have to be ready to improvise, to riff. In music, and in the traveling my wife and I do, I've always been up for new things. But this school change really threw me at the beginning. I've been thinking about why that was, and about change in general. I'm still not 100% sold on

the textbook (more like 90%), but at our last faculty
meeting we all agreed that the curriculum is
obviously working. The students are performing
well and applying their new skills with confidence
and enthusiasm. This old teacher has learned something new—el cambio es bueno!

Stage Priority: Understanding the Change in a Deeper Way

Primed for learning in Stage 5, you break through to a
deeper understanding of the change and its benefits. Part
of this understanding comes naturally—there is a rhythm
to what you assimilate as you move through the six stages,
and here is a point where you see through to another level.
But in Stage 5, you also *actively* seek to map the change
from all sides with understanding—through things like
after-action reports, group discussions, your own private
reflection, and more.

After that? You integrate this understanding with the
rest of your life—with your memories of prior work and
life changes, with your present, with your goals and vision
for the future. What you've learned becomes an integral
part of you. That's when you're in Stage 6.

Acknowledgment's Value

If self-esteem is good in an organizational setting, cockiness
not so good, it follows that doing some acknowledging at
this stage should have benefits. That you're ready to do this
is another sign of your progress. Acknowledgment builds

in more self-awareness. It builds in engagement. Acknowledge the distance you've traveled. Acknowledge that your hard work is paying off. Acknowledge those who helped you, and the fact that your early vision of the change was not as clear as it is now. Acknowledge things to do better, things you'll never do again.

Acknowledge things you've done right.

In almost every area of high human achievement, whether in sports, the arts, even chess, new studies are showing that practice, reinforcement, dedication, and support are even more vital than we thought. Obviously inborn talent plays a role, but the idea that people are simply "born to be great" grows less convincing the more it is studied. The chess whiz, the teenage violinist, the power forward, and the like, not only log much more time learning their craft than others, they've also discovered ways to "learn deeper." They've discovered better reinforcement methods. What does this have to do with acknowledgment? Acknowledging is a form of self-reinforcement. It deepens learning. So go ahead, do some acknowledging. And, if you like, a little celebrating, too. You've earned it.

Learning Curves

For eighteen years I was book-page editor for a Sunbelt newspaper. I'd been with this paper since graduating journalism school. I began as a courts reporter, moved to features, and, being a book lover, jumped to books when the position opened up.

I loved my job. I wrote a column, assigned reviews, interviewed writers, sat on literary awards panels,

and every year traveled to our big annual book-indus-
try convention. Four months ago, pretty much out of
the blue, in a cost-cutting move, my position was
dropped. The paper shrunk the Sunday book section
from two pages to one and now runs only wire-serv-
ice reviews. Readers called and wrote to protest, and
two local authors I'd championed over the years
wrote eloquent (and sharp) letters, but to no avail.

My final day came, and I cleared the last clutter
from my cubicle (yes, still a cubicle), said some
goodbyes, then said more goodbyes at a party that
evening. Needless to say, I would have liked if my
employers had taken a stand for our city's book
culture, but I also understand a newspaper is a
business, and a difficult one these days. A book-page
editor for a newspaper of 150,000 subscribers—
fewer and fewer reading books—is dispensable.

Having edited my section right up until the last
day, I hadn't had much time to mope and brood. I
started that the next day. But I was also telling
myself now I finally had time to start that novel I'd
always wanted to write. But when I sat down at my
home computer I was doing more staring into space
than anything else. Then one day I saw a notice in
the employment pages looking for someone to
teach two composition classes at the local community
college. Thinking it might get me out of my funk, I
put together a resume and e-mailed it over. Three
weeks later, I was teaching the classes. And that
very first weekend after starting teaching, I started
making some progress on my idea for a novel.

The teaching position is temporary (the regular instructor is on sick leave). And it could be months before I'll be able to tell if my novel-writing is time well spent. I'll also say I miss my old job, my colleagues. But I'm enjoying getting students excited about writing, and I feel as productive as I've ever been. The measure of anger I had at my newspaper is mostly gone, and already I'm able to drive past my former workplace without feeling a big pang. I'm learning new things about myself (who knew I could be something of a ham in a classroom?), and I feel good about seeing if I have any talent for this craft that I have always had so much respect for and spent years promoting at the paper. I'm not exactly sure what the future holds, but I'm happy to be moving forward, not stuck dwelling on the past.

Stay on the Learning Road

In the Discomfort stage, you pursued ways of energizing yourself, even if it was something as simple as taking a new route to work. Here, take time to reflect on your own experience with learning. And consider learning something new outside work, or deepening what you know of something, to complement your work learning. Why? To stay mentally limber. To reinforce your learning habit, which will help you in rounding off your work change and prepare you for coming changes. Our brains were made for learning, no matter how many decades we have under our belts. The research is clear—a learning brain is a healthy one.

Consider your own education: what helped you learn best? Who were your best teachers, and why? If you have school-age children, no doubt education is never far from your mind. As you watch your children learn, and as you teach them, reflect on your own recent change: training-wise, what was successful? Have you needed to do any other kinds of new learning recently? Maybe it's simply a new computer program. What worked?

Is there some craft, some sport, some home-improvement step you'd like to learn? Is there a book or magazine with interesting knowledge you'd like to acquire? What about listening to an audio book explor-ing some corner of history or politics or science while you commute? Maybe you used to do crossword puz-zles years ago—why not restart? Or how about dipping into a little of the foreign language you took in high school or college. Learn a word a day. Or just a word a week. They still add up. *Pauciloquy*—know what it means? We didn't until reading Annie Dillard's new novel. It means "brevity in speech." You wish we'd learned this sooner, huh?

The point is, keep feeding your mind. The change has just given your mental muscles a workout—they're stronger. Exercise them as often you can. Maintain their strength.

Reel Learning

To deepen thinking about learning, you need not run to the education-research bookshelf. There are a number of memorable movies focusing on what makes a good teacher or mentor, what gets students (of all ages) motivated, what makes a special student. Watch any one of these one night or on a weekend, and you'll find yourself doing . . . pedagogical reflection. (*Pedagogical:* "of, relating to, or befitting a teacher or education.")

Here are some movies that fit the bill:

▽ *A Beautiful Mind* (Russell Crowe, 2001)

▽ *Akeelah and the Bee* (Angela Bassett, Laurence Fishburne, 2006)

▽ *The Browning Version* (Albert Finney, 1994)

▽ *Educating Rita* (Michael Caine, 1983)

▽ *The Dead Poets Society* (Robin Williams, 1989)

▽ *Freedom Writers* (Hillary Swank, 2007)

▽ *Good Will Hunting* (Matt Damon, Ben Affleck, Robin Williams, 1997)

▽ *Mr. Holland's Opus* (Richard Dreyfus, 1995)

We might also mention three documentaries: *Spellbound*, *Wordplay*, and *Hoop Dreams*. The first is about the national spelling-bee competition, the second is about crossword fanatics, and the third, our wild-card choice, is about two youngsters from inner-city Chicago, gifted basketball players who are learning about the game and sports in America. And learning about life. One of their mothers is also attending school at night, and in one unforgettable scene she literally jumps for joy at a good grade.

Just looking at her face you can see the reinforcement setting in.

Change Lessons

With an eye to getting this particular change experience to pay guidance dividends down the road, you want to maximize your learning—you want to absorb as many lessons as you can. It helps to make this a conscious goal, which is what some of the preceding has been about. Of course your organization is also going to want to maximize learning. Management should formalize an employee-feedback process to ascertain what channels and formats communicated best, what made learning the new stuff easiest.

Highlight what was successful. What needs tinkering?

Whether sharing orally in meetings, through survey sheets, conferencing, or via e-mail, now is the time to have a company's people reflect on the recent learning and training. Lessons compiled will be a valuable feature in any kind of change after-action report.

Choose your query language and modes carefully, however. Anyone who has ever focus-grouped something has seen this happen. A room of people, asked to "critique" things, to list what they "didn't like" or what they thought "didn't work," will dutifully, even zealously, set to work sifting for perceived flaws in every direction, on occasion going right back into early-stage negative thinking that for some will last. Gathering info is good—a gripe-hour, not so good.

Sometimes simply asking for in-depth feedback on "what worked," or where process "positives" became clear, is sufficient—the process of elimination tells you what can be improved.

The Rearview Mirror Trap

An after-action report, whether formally representing the collective findings of a team, unit, division, or company, or whether simply the guided reflections of an individual employee (even just a "memo to self"), is one thing; *fixating on the past* is another. Just as avoiding ego-inflation is important in Stage 5, so is being careful that looking back doesn't grow into excessive rumination. Now that the change has become the new reality, now that you have a moment to breathe, some people find themselves looking back more than is helpful. Are you almost too good at identifying your mistakes? Okay, you're equal to the change but has your mind been drifting back to the start of the process and starting a whole new round of inner criticism about why the thing had to happen in the first place? Nothing wrong with looking into the rearview mirror as you move. Unless, that is, you look too long, or the mirror's angle needs adjusting.

The trick is to balance identification of missteps with recognition of strengths to build on. This goes for company-level retrospection as well. A backward look is smart and essential up to the point where it becomes deficit-vision—the road ahead full of traffic and twists.

Case in Point: Big Table Eats Catering

I grew up in New Orleans. I went north for college and business school, then returned and opened a catering business—Big Table Eats—geared to serving one of the city's biggest growth industries at the time: film production. Thanks to a series of innovative state and local tax credits, we were attracting more movie shoots than any city other than Los Angeles. A lot of people needed to be fed—people used to high-quality gourmet catering.

I secured a facility, bought trucks, hired chefs. I tripled my staff that first year. We delivered food to location shoots, soundstages, and wrap parties. Before long, set managers were calling me months ahead of time to secure service. The next year, business was even better. An actor whose name you'd know, one of my first customers, was back in town, filming another movie. He said he'd come back for our food. Then Hurricane Katrina hit. In terms of physical damage, it could have been worse. We had to repair—not rebuild—our facility; we lost a truck. But some of my staff were homeless and later left the state. Our best chef moved to San Francisco. And the two big movie productions we were servicing relocated, one to Baton Rouge, the other L.A.

I was pretty much numb those first couple weeks. I was trying to help my staff, trying to determine if we'd have any business that autumn. I realized pretty quickly we would not—at least not in southern Louisiana. I met with each of my employees, or spoke to them by phone if they'd left town. I wanted to hear their thoughts, their plans for the future. Each morning, in a pocket notebook, I made a list of what I called "The 3's": the three most important things to do that day.

Three key people to consult (from staff to insurance and bank contacts to movie production managers in L.A. and New York). Three ways I could adapt my business. We were going to regroup. That was the plan.

Relocating my business to Baton Rouge for the fall was the big decision. I kept all staff who wanted to make the move and ended up hiring more people up there. We continued servicing the shoot that had shifted there, and we picked up two more productions, a TV show and a small-budget movie. It wasn't easy but we made it through autumn.

We're now in both places: Baton Rouge and New Orleans. Even combined, we're not where we were before Katrina business-wise but we're making it. I have more overhead costs with two facilities, but productions have been pretty steady upstate and business is returning here as well. Some of it's small, like documentary shoots. We also cater to some national news crews and do VIP catering when politicians and so forth come to town. The Saints are now a client, and during the season we serve opposing teams as well.

Turnover's been minimal this year. I'm still working with some people who have been with me since day one. I'm so grateful for their efforts, their skills, their commitment. The anger I had after the storm is not entirely gone but it doesn't squeeze me anymore. Right now I'm feeling pretty optimistic. Both about my business and our city. I feel like I've learned a lifetime of lessons about how to adapt, what people can bounce back from. I feel confident that no matter what happens down the road, I'll be able to land on my feet. I've also learned some things about myself—how I am in a crisis, that no matter how sad or bad I feel, I don't sink all the way into despair, I never really lose hope. No one can predict the future, obviously, but I think my business is here to stay and is only going to get better.

In Stage 5, you're able to rather clearly identify some short-term "features" of the change and some longer-term "benefits." Features add to your present motivation, and your insight into longer-haul benefits informs your decision-making and your vision of the future.

All that remains is to turn your understanding into wisdom.

Things to welcome and avoid have to do with making the most of your deep learning.

Things to Avoid in Stage 5

▽ **Believing you've learned enough**

Chances are, even with this particular change, there's more to know, more to get better at. Enjoy this feeling of competence, but ask yourself whether you know "all."

▽ **Captiousness**

The fact that there's even a word for "a tendency to point out trivial faults" tells you that the thing exists. Identify what needs correcting—then move on.

▽ **Keeping your understanding to yourself**

Not everyone might be as up to speed as you. Since "we're all in this together," look for opportunities to bring others along with your grasp of the workplace change.

What to Welcome

▽ **Initiative**

The creative autonomy you experience in Stage 4 should keep paying off here as well.

▽ **Desires to "take stock" of the change and understand new aspects of the job**

Both things are good—one involving looking back and gleaning lessons, the other involving looking forward to take full advantage of this learning mode.

▽ **A willingness to teach and lead**

Knowledge communicated by and among employees grows deep cognitive roots.

Keys to Moving On

▽ Harmonize your change-learning and self-learning

▽ Identify the change's long-term benefits

▽ Ask, "What else can I learn to be even more productive?"

"Flow"

Learning—it happens here. The lasting kind. Of course ever since the change was announced, you've been absorbing new information. But here the picture of both the change and the way you best deal with change is fully internalized; job competence and self-knowledge lock into place and if mastery is too strong a word, then perhaps "flow" is appropriate, that term in performance psychology for when you no longer have to *think* but simply do. Athletes call it being "in the zone." What you need to do your job is in your bones.

In the green stages, you have flow.

When you turn the page, you reach Stage 6. There's something almost mysterious that happens in Stage 5, something almost alchemical, where all that you've learned about the change and about yourself begins blending together. When this blending is complete, you're ready for Integration, the last stage of The Change Cycle. To help this blending, it helps to focus on what you have identified as positive features of the change and to focus on what the change has helped you understand about yourself. Maybe it's the way this change has led to some changes inside you—in your vision of things, your perspective on work and life. Understanding is peaking now, and some of the things you understand will be of assistance for a very long time.

Are you ready? Go ahead. The light is green.

Note to Self:

I understand. I'm ready. I'm *moving!*

Chapter Six

Change Moves Me

It's what you learn after you know it all that counts.

John Wooden

Stage 6: Experiencing Integration

To come this far, to assimilate a change, means you've demonstrated adaptability. But just as we might locate wisdom a notch above understanding, so there's a resourceful orientation that occupies a spot above adaptability: flexibility. *What doesn't bend will break,* it's been said. Flexibility is vital both for individuals experiencing change and of course for the company as a whole. It's more than durability. It means ever-present open-mindedness—an openness to learning, receiving, and giving. To understand flexibility in a change context is to understand that resiliency can have more impact than strength.

When you are flexible, you influence the *potentials*. The potential to turn a disappointment into an opportunity. The potential to turn what appeared to be a failure into an achievement—and a step toward even more success. Having moved through The Change Cycle, you've experienced firsthand how bending at the right points and accepting forward motion prove more conducive to productivity than stubbornly trying to wait out the transition. This is why choosing change is much more resourceful than risking change choosing you.

With any luck, you will carry forward this flexibility lesson—and it will serve you down the road. Hold up and highlight what you've learned, consciously; it will establish a place in your memory you can draw on when needed. You will remember a time when it seemed that things at work had taken a turn for the bad, or at least the far from ideal. And not only that, the thicket of difficulties seemed permanent. But by managing those early feelings, and stepping through to new perspectives, and bending at times but never breaking, you made it.

What Is Found at Journey's End

A question: When you encountered the word *wisdom* here and in the previous chapter, did it give you any kind of pause? It's not a word to throw around lightly. Were you curious to see how it applied? Did you perhaps think, *Wisdom, eh? I can see how it might apply to some people, on their change journey, but not sure about mine.*

I'm okay with "learning" and "knowledge" and "under-
standing." Though even that last one's a pretty big word.

Well, we're going to agree. About wisdom. Up to a
point. Just as there's a broad range of work changes people can be hit with, from a minor procedural shift to sudden job loss or the effects of a natural disaster like a
hurricane, there's variance in the amount of insight people acquire and the growth they undergo as they cycle
through the six stages. The world would be a different
place if all it took to create a wise man or woman—a
sage—was enduring a professional change. We'd have
sages all over the place.

Still, you've come a distance, no matter the change. And
let's face it, when you're in a change, especially at the start,
it doesn't feel small. Think back: the anxiety and feeling
of powerlessness were real. The anger (if you felt anger)
was real. The dread (if you felt dread) was real. Then all
the adjusting and familiarizing and coping and seeking of
energy. The information hunt. The up and down. And par-
allel to the up and down, your efforts to understand yourself in change—your work of self-knowledge—so you
could move out of the red and yellow stages into green.
The learning you did. The discovering.

Did you acquire wisdom? Only you can answer that.
But the remainder of this chapter will explore what it
means to reach the knowing, even philosophical, state of
mind that is Stage 6, *Integration*. Here you integrate all
you've learned, some of it even becoming second nature,
which gives it utility forever. You'll finish chapter and book
carrying forward a greater acceptance and understanding
of the change process—and a greater understanding of

yourself. Are you wiser? Well, we'll say this: Every wisdom tradition we know believes in the value of a journey. For a simple, timeless reason—journeys teach you about life, and about yourself. You've just been on a journey. It's almost over. You're not there yet, but you're close. You're very close.

How We Feel in Stage 6: Satisfied

If pure unadulterated bliss is asking too much of Stage 6, how does contentment sound? A state of well-being. Satisfaction at having made it through the change. Thinking of how our work paid off, we feel contentment. We feel contentment thinking we could do it again, maybe even better. We feel contentment at having proved ourselves change-resilient.

This attitude may be company-wide. We've done it. We're a change-resilient company.

We've not only survived, we're starting to thrive.

Individually, we like the idea that going forward we'll be better able to face work newness as possibility rather than as threat or loss. And maybe newness in life, too. We're pleased to look around and see some of our fellow workers enjoying end-of-cycle satisfaction as well. Our content gaze also takes note of which company features (policies, procedures, technology, communication strategies, leadership moves) helped make the change work. Of course we don't ignore what didn't work. But right now, we're about positives.

We feel connected to the people we work with. What psychologists call the "social emotions" have a heightened presence in the green stages. Camaraderie, collegiality, generosity. And empathy, the ability to better feel what another is feeling. Just as we take pleasure in the contentment of our fellow Stage 6 travelers, so we also feel concern for those who might not have progressed as quickly. We want to help them along.

Is there anything to trip us up? Conceit and complacency. More on this shortly.

For now, enjoy the feeling of a job well done.

How We Think in Stage 6: Focused

We think "philosophically." What does this entail? It's higher-order thinking, reflection without the wobbles and bumps of reactive emotion. We don't get hung up on the small stuff. It's not that we ignore details, it's that we process specifics efficiently, without losing sight of the long view. Principles guide our thinking. Fairness, justice, and honesty matter to us, in the workplace, in the way our company operates. It's not all about serving self.

At the executive level, Stage 6 thinking means being fair to those impacted by a change they may have had no say over. It means no one in the company will be forgotten. The philanthropic impulse may increase in organizations experiencing Stage 6 satisfaction.

At all company levels, our reflections may well extend beyond work. We think about our lives, the balance between our work and life, what we prioritize, what we cherish. No longer scrambling for more information or buried under a million new work details every day, we do more thinking about the meaning of things. We focus on what matters.

If we took stock of the change in Stage 5, here we might take stock of our life.

Managers and leaders, fear not—Stage 6 is not purely philosophic, every employee a sandaled Plato (or Soren Kierkegaard—with Birkenstocks). The big thoughts take place during the commute, in the evenings, on weekends. "Integrated" workers work, they save thoughts of truth, beauty and the good for after hours (or before). In fact, while on the job the Stage 6 mind is capable of laser-like focus. We hear this often: people say the thing they like most about the Integration stage is the mental acuity, the crisp concentration.

Even while multitasking, their minds stay clear.

And when off work, they have energy left over to ponder the universe.

Now that's a stage.

How We Act in Stage 6: Generous

Along with our sharp, productive work performance, we also find ourselves saluting the efforts of others and assisting those who need it. It's not that Stage 6 turns everyone into saints, but those elevated social emotions and our broad outlook incline us to actions more often closer to generous than egoistic. Is it unusual to be speaking of generous acts in a book addressing changes in a corporate setting? Perhaps not as unusual as one might instinctively think. Would a company really thrive if its "philosophy," such as it is, consisted entirely of preaching the gospel of profits-above-all, individualism, and "greed is good"?

The Change Cycle model has developed over years of hearing employees tell us what it is like when a work transition seems fully integrated into their lives, when it becomes the new normal. They report experiencing what we might call an expanded spirit. They feel more themselves, and this self tends to be more open-hearted than early in the change when they felt confused, overwhelmed, stressed—in a kind of fight for clarity and safety.

So if not out-and-out generosity, a heightened sense of togetherness and responsibility for others is present. For some, there is even a desire to "give back"—to colleagues, to the organization. Early in the change process, this kind of wish would have seemed hard to imagine.

Another thing shaping our Stage 6 actions is the inclination to keep on improving—not just our own performance but the organization's as a whole. The driver behind this goal is rather basic: namely, when things are going well, we often want them to go even better. Success breeds a desire for more success. Suddenly we think, *Let's get to Stage 6 2.0.*

Directing our gaze toward the future, we start working on things that will not only make the most out of this change but will better support transitions in the future.

Case in Point: St. Rose Roasters

I worked ten different kinds of jobs before my sister and I started a coffee company fifteen years ago. We got lucky with timing as people's taste for quality-bean coffee was just starting to take off around then.

A few years after that the rise of online shopping helped get us mail-order customers all over America. Before coffee, I sold futons. I was a head waiter for four years. I opened a bar-laundromat. And my sister and I ran a custom stereo-speaker business.

Our coffee company started with three employees and now employs close to a hundred. We run five St. Rose cafes in addition to our flagship store and cafe, at the rear of which is our production facility. We purchase beans from Mexico, South America, Jamaica, Africa, and Indonesia. My sister and I travel around the world, meeting with growers and shippers, attending "coffee summits." We just broke ground for a new facility, which will double the size of our present one. This year a regional airline selected us as their coffee supplier—the paper cups bear our company name!

But almost every day a moment comes when I remember all my previous jobs—so many years of trying this, trying that. I even sold crepes from a cart one summer. Forgot to mention that. I'm proud of our success, of course. My sister and I have worked hard to get where we are. But I also realize things could have turned out differently. We rode a pair of trends I'd love to claim we anticipated in full, but in fact we did not. We went with our instincts and things happened to work out. Early on we put an emphasis on thinking "green" (using recycled paper, making sure our facility had bike access, etc.) and this, too, ended up serving the company well—today more than ever. We have employees who believe in the company and we believe in them—our health plan, child-care facilities, and other policies reflect this belief. Our company also buys a lot of "fair trade" beans. Fair trade coffee programs are designed to empower small-scale farmers in developing countries, partly by putting more money in their pockets rather than in the pockets of intermediaries who traditionally have taken advantage of them. Our purchase patterns encourage sustainable coffee-production processes, which not only support small-farmer security over the long term but also improve coffee quality and consistency.

Our company continues to evolve as global coffee-growing changes, as the global coffee economy changes, as things change here at home. Nothing is static, not marketing, not our Internet selling, not our management-employee coordination. We work closely with the city, which has been good to us—we want to do right by them. It's not about brownie points or corporate citizen awards or whatever. It's about respecting the people who make our company work, whether it's the cafe baristas, the bean-roasters, the pickers, or the shippers. My sister and I had some basic beliefs about how to run a business coming in, and we've tried to keep faith with these beliefs. So far, at least for us, it has worked out.

Stage 6 Priority: Flexibility

Nothing is static. The words are worthy of being carved onto the twenty-first-century equivalent of the Delphic temple in Ancient Greece. Words to live by. Words to work by. And there's no more effective way of orienting oneself in a ceaselessly changing world than by understanding the art of flexibility—and by practicing it at every turn. This includes even the way you *talk* about the world—and about work and yourself. Whenever possible, try to practice *flexible self-talk*. Make flexible responses part of your internal dialogue. Coaching of this sort does affect attitude and behavior. Use the same language in your work exchanges. Often—especially when it comes to taking on a challenge or integrating a change—flex-talk imprints as firmly or more firmly on you, the speaker, than it does on the colleague in your exchange.

To Know More, Notice More

Rigid Talk	Flex Talk
"This just creates problems."	"How can I make this work?"
"I'm being taken advantage of."	"What can I offer this situation?"
"This probably means something bad."	"This might lead to something good."
"This situation stinks."	"How will I feel about this in a week?"
"They forced my hand."	"I need to learn more before I take action."
"This is ruining my day."	"I'm responsible for how I handle this."

We mentioned conceit as one of the two Stage 6 traps (the other being complacency). Ego inflation emerges as a possible problem in the Understanding stage and continues here. The fully integrated employee—the person at journey's end, the change road traveled—does not claim excessive credit, insist others would do best to follow his or her lead, or criticize those who have a different view or who are still working their way forward. Of course behind many displays of arrogance is often a core lack of confidence or a narcissistic need for constant validation. These individuals haven't found the quiet contentment that marks true Stage 6 arrival.

Less Than Integrated	Integrated
Nonresponsive to shifting work environment	Takes advantage of growth opportunities
Does things their own way no matter what	Accepts advice; offers help to others
Spotlights their own role in success	Thanks others for the collective effort
Points to the failures of colleagues	Neither overlooks nor harps on mistakes
"Just call me Super Changer!"	"I'm happy how this turned out."
"It doesn't need any more tweaking."	"If we need to adjust, no problem."
"They should be learning from me."	"I've grown through this."
"Why would I want to do that?"	"What can I contribute?"

Learning Curves

Daniel, an entrepreneur who began in sales, was instrumental in merging the company he helped lead with a long-established but now under-performing firm. He'd bought and turned around two other distressed companies in the past. There were some clashes of opinion and a protracted merger process, but once complete, Daniel moved full steam ahead into finding and landing new clients for his new company.

However, while he searched the market for more business, disaffection and confusion was growing at both the management and staff levels. This turmoil was caused by issues ranging from uncertain salaries to remade job descriptions. Daniel directed others to work on these issues, and when progress was not rapid he openly criticized people.

Having made his point, he went back to focusing his attention on grabbing accounts. He put into this activity the same kind of detailed, dynamic effort he had given his selling of the merger benefits and the negotiating of its terms, including the terms of his own contract. During coming months, though, he watched two managing partners, four directors, and twelve staffers leave the company. In exit interviews, a common thread was the lack of consideration given those who had worked for years for the two companies pre-merger. Rather than marketing the new company, Daniel soon found himself constantly responding to volatile exits and vacant positions.

Rather quickly, profits began to shrink. Daniel's solution?

"We just have to hire better people," he explained. "People who actually want to work for this company. Who said it was going to be easy?"

A year later, the company was still struggling.

Complacency Challenge

As we said, for most people, given the right work culture, seeing things work during a change increases their drive—adds to their ambition—to make things work even better. The energy and confidence—they're there. But this doesn't mean that under certain circumstances complacency can't set in. Over time *We did it!* can turn into *It's good enough.* Or worse, *Look—it's still great! Great great great! Isn't it great?*

There must be some classic myth or fable expressing the dangers of excessive admiration. Gaze too long upon your handiwork and . . . something bad happens.

So just as it's wise and necessary to mark progress and even to take the time to celebrate it, so is it wise to be mindful of this Stage 6 trap: laurel-resting. Everyone has a stake in avoiding this. While seeking that proper balance between affirming success and identifying missteps, managers and leaders will be on-watch for signs of complacency and may keep the word itself—the C-word—in active workplace circulation. Again, language has impact. Speak the name of this thing to be avoided and people will run self-checks.

Above and beyond this, here are ways for managers and leaders to keep themselves forward-leaning and to keep the company as a whole out of the Complacency Zone:

▽ **Reevaluate and reprioritize**
The change brought certain company strengths and weaknesses into focus. Your perspective on the company's relation to the market, to competitors—it's changed. Now is a good time to use this new lens to evaluate goals, practices, and priorities.

▽ **Initiate systemic and structural development to better support future transitions**
Change educates. You now know the company better than ever. What needs to be put in place to keep the company or organization resilient and flexible for the next change?

▽ **Hold planning sessions for future pacing**
Involve the whole company. These sessions keep people looking forward, help them find value in change-anticipation, and pioneer ground-level ideas. Without the threat of imminence or set time-frames, these meetings help minds start to adjust for the next change.

▽ **Design ways to close skill gaps for the next change implementation**
What should the company and its people be better at next time around?

▽ **Distribute authority, accountability, and responsibility**
The change process uncovers employees with talents for mentoring and leadership. Encourage them. Empower those skilled and ready for it to take on more authority and responsibility.

▽ **Promote the learning of new or advanced work skills**
Employees remain in active-learning mode. Anything that helps them harness this expands their work scope and keeps the company energized. Noncomplacent.

▽ **Provide personal-enhancement training programs**
Green-stage employees seek ways to grow, to know, to do and see more, both at work and at home. A creative company culture can encourage this seeking. Always-learning employees are dynamic, interested, and motivated. They help keep companies change-resilient.

Wisdom in Change

People grow, come into greater understanding, and integrate larger lessons about life or work in ways both unplanned and by design, in ways both accidental and by effort. Sometimes things just happen to us, we weather them or muddle through, and come out the other side realizing we've learned some important things that will be with us always. Other times, in ways both large and small, we actively seek the kind of higher understanding that we commonly call wisdom.

Think of people who spend months traveling exotic lands alone or sail an ocean solo or go on a retreat. Even adventures that feature great physical challenges often involve another element: the person wants to come back in some way wiser, a changed person. There are much smaller ways to tap into this kind of experience. Often it is simply a book. You read the life story of someone you find inspirational, perhaps someone who came from very little or faced a lot of hardship. The narrative is absorbing, but you also find yourself thinking about things: about the world, your life. A great novel can do this. A great film. A Shakespeare play. How about a book written by someone who traveled exotic lands alone, questing, actively looking to grow? The author of the best-selling *Eat, Pray, Love* did just that.

The point is, you've just been through something, you made it, you're back, and you might be feeling not only halfway content but also a little inquisitive, ready for insight. Your mode is "big picture." Why not capitalize and seek out a little wisdom (or just something approaching it—a wisdom seed) while you're at it? It may be a biography or a book by someone you consider wise. It may be a book from a religious or philosophical tradition. Poetry. Sometimes reading just a few pages plants a seed. Anything along these lines you take in right now will provide reinforcement. It will help the mind process and store the big lessons.

Does music get you thinking? How about a long walk? A weekend drive?

Know thyself, said Ancient Greek philosopher Socrates. You've been trying to do some of that lately. Self-knowledge—it ranks high with most of our time-tested thinkers. As does a clear-eyed sense of the world as a place where change can happen at any moment. A place where there are things you can't control, and others you can. Where you can know some things, but not other things. Where sometimes you are exactly right, and sometimes you can err.

Because you are human.

Your sense of the world as just this kind of place has been sharpened and deepened lately. Anything that touches on this sense with understanding will resonate right now.

"Toggle-Vision"

In Stage 5, you did your share of looking back, of taking stock. The time felt right to survey the change process, to chart what went on in terms of both successes and glitches, and in terms of both your company's and your own forward motion. In Integration, you are free, and greatly motivated, to gaze into the future, both near and far. The future of your job, the future of your company or organization, the future of the business you are in. Your gaze is clear and steady. In Stage 6, you're charting—you're assessing—present, past, and future as well:

> *What do I need to do now to get me to where I want to be in the future?*
>
> *If the company moves this way, where will it be a year out? Two years? Five?*
>
> *Next change we won't do that thing we did last change.*

Easily, fluidly, your mind in Stage 6 not only sweeps forward in time, calculating, envisioning, but also ranges back into the near and far past and just as swiftly assesses the present. Call it "toggle-vision." It's part of the integration you enjoy here at change's end. Your big-picture sense, your sense of the landscape, applies to time as well.

Past, present, future—like that jigsaw puzzle, it's one complete whole now, readily scanned, no piece distractedly out of place. It's liberating. Thoughts of the change, even those early, less-than-delightful moments, don't weigh you down. And you face the future confidently, squarely.

New-Model Schema

Remember the word *schema* from early in the book? It's that complex or nexus of thoughts, feelings, memories, and expectations gathered around some potent aspect of human life. A potent aspect like . . . change. We all enter a work or life change with a certain schema, and it may or may not serve us well. Change, as you might imagine, has a way of generating some pretty gloomy schemas, right up there with death and taxes. These schemas stick around, as is, unless we make some deliberate effort to reshape them, or go through some experience with enough remodeling force. Here, both things happened. A change worked on us. And we worked on being as knowing and aware as we could during the change, with an eye to moving through the cycle and emerging better prepared for the next change.

And so you have. Your change schema has changed. Next change, you will likely still experience some loss, perhaps some anger, almost surely some anxiety, a dash or maybe more than a dash of doubt and discomfort, but you will know these things are coming, you will have ways of dealing with them, and you will know more fully and surely than before that they will pass. *This will pass.* And you will know Discovery is coming too, and with it energy, and after that the calm of Understanding, followed by the vision and contentment of Integration. And you will know to never expect to absolutely love the next change, although theoretically it could happen (maybe). You will also know that the next time you go through The Change Cycle you will be even better prepared for the cycle after that.

You will know one more thing after closing this book. You will know another change will come. They always do. At work. In life. Another change will come.

But you'll be ready for it. In fact, you're ready now.

Note to Self:

The Chinese word for change is *wei ji*.
It means two things.
Crisis and opportunity.
That bears repeating.
Wei ji. Crisis and opportunity.

Change Beliefs

During the summer we wrote this book, an extraordinary thing happened in the game of professional baseball, a story brought to our attention by more than one friend. A former top pitcher for the St. Louis Cardinals named Rick Ankiel returned to his team after several years in the minor leagues. That in itself is not so extraordinary. It is what Ankiel did, the position he played, and how well he performed upon his return that amazes.

He did not return as a pitcher, but rather as an outfielder. He was an elite big-league pitcher until he began experiencing problems controlling his legendary fastball. All his life he had been doing this thing wonderfully well, and suddenly something was going terribly wrong. He would try to throw the ball toward home plate and it would fly out of his hand, soaring ten feet over the catcher's head, or ten feet to the left. The harder he tried to throw it straight, the worse his accuracy became. He even had an episode in a World Series game. Wild pitch after wild pitch. And nothing was wrong with his arm.

He saw a number of sports psychologists. He tried everything. Nothing worked. His career looked to be over. This world-class gift of his had turned into a curse.

But he did not give up. He adapted, and in a way baseball experts say has never quite been seen before. He was always a good hitter, especially for a man who came up as a pitcher, and he was a great athlete overall. Vowing

171

to work his way back to his team, he went down to the minor leagues and before long was doing well as an outfielder. But still—would he be able to make it all the way back to the Cardinals, playing a different position? Would he be able to endure this much change and still perform at a top level?

His ex-teammates had faith. His former manager had faith. If anyone can do this, Rick can, they said. Though deep in their hearts, surely they had doubts.

He rejoined his former teammates and manager in midsummer. In his first game he hit a home run. In his second game he hit two home runs. His manager got emotional talking to the press after that first game. He'd seen all the up and down, the struggle.

Rick Ankiel kept on hitting home runs. He helped his team climb up the standings. It's pretty clear he was the central reason for their sudden winning ways.

It's a great change story. It's inspirational. There are a lot of these stories out there, if you look for them, if you value them. And it helps to value them—they are a ready resource when the going gets rough, in your work or in your life.

And though we can't—and wouldn't want to—state plainly that at some time at some point ahead, the going will get rough again, we can state plainly this: Change will come again, as day follows night. And when it does, you have a map, tools, skills, and experience—you have The Change Cycle—available for guidance. Will it make your change easy? Unlikely. Will it make your change *easier*—to manage, to integrate, and to learn from? Yes. That we are happy to state plainly as well.

Working through your change with the awareness The Change Cycle brings can actually improve your overall attitude toward change. Understanding the stages and putting into practice the navigation insights in this book can help you lift Change from the "Oh no" box and drop it into the "I can deal" folder. Rumor has it there are people who have never filed Change in an "Oh no" box. Just a rumor. Most of us are pretty happy for an attitude improvement, when it comes to change.

In our change management trainings, we make reference to the story of the late actor Christopher Reeve. We use it as an illustration of how much change we can endure and still retain our spirit. And not only that: how we can still be productive.

Mr. Reeve, following the riding accident that left him quadriplegic, would no longer be a leading man in Hollywood movies. No longer was he Superman. But he accepted a new calling: fighting for better treatment—and perhaps some day a cure—for paralysis.

Stories like those of Christopher Reeve and Rick Ankiel stay in the mind. They not only inspire but can bring perspective to situations where we might be struggling for a proper way of measuring some newness, whether a crisis or something that at first looked like a crisis but turned out to be something less in the light of day (or in the light of calmer assessment). We all have our balance-bringing stories, just as we all have core beliefs about change. Christopher Reeve would have had his own stories and beliefs, and they served him well. Same for Rick Ankiel—he was drawing on accounts he'd heard, plus his guiding beliefs about change.

It can be valuable to inventory these beliefs, to articulate and consider them. As authors of a book about change and veterans of many years on the change playing field, we thought we might leave you with an inventory of our own beliefs. When we're tired of change, these beliefs help refocus us. Perhaps they will be of some worth to you as well.

Our Change Beliefs

Change Just Happens—We Don't Need to Take It Personally

Our work experiences have taught us that organizational change sometimes means untimely, unfortunate, even bad things can happen to good people. It is a fact of work life. We believe playing *What if?* and *They should . . .* squanders energy that could serve us better in other ways. There are no gold stars for holding on to a victim mentality. It's not what happens to us, but how we react and respond to it that counts. We can't control change. We can only control and handle ourselves, personally and professionally.

Work Change Has the Potential to Bring Out the Best in People

This potential may not appear right away, or even for a while, and it may be very hard to believe in at the onset of the change. But we have seen it happen. Again and again.

There Is No Right Way to Do the Wrong Thing

There have been times when change has gotten the best of us. In our worst blaming, angry moments, we have deceived ourselves into believing that revenge, antipathy, and other assorted flavors of negative and immature behavior were justified. We were wrong.

It's Important to Take Responsibility for What We Have Created in Our Lives—Both the Good and the Bad

We believe in owning responsibility for the way we handle change. We believe how we react and respond to life's changes reflects our emotional health and maturity. We believe in asking, *Am I trying to find my way or lose my temper? Do I want to "be right" or "get right"? Is my ego or is my good sense going to have the final word?* Our attitude in change is either the key to a locked door, or a spring that makes an open door slam in our faces. It's our responsibility to choose well.

To go with our change beliefs, we also try to keep in mind five more things:

▽ We are able to learn from every work experience.

▽ We need to consider communication issues from a broad perspective and with an open mind.

▽ If we must assume something, we assume there is something we don't know.

▽ We will take the appropriate action when we know what it is.

And finally:

▽ If it's going to be a little bit funny in the future, it must be a little bit funny now.

Our aim is to have these pointers guide us in the way we live our professional lives. We would like them to be habits, like brushing our teeth. But of course they do not always come so easily or automatically. So we try to stay alert and run some checks.

And we strive to remember always that . . . *change moves us.*

Index

Acknowledgments

At the root of this work are the people of South Africa in the years before and since apartheid. Their struggles to change, their courage to move forward, and their faith in the human spirit helped inspire this work in the beginning. We are grateful to have witnessed one of the greatest change efforts ever made by a country—its citizens, organizations, communities, and local governments. We are so honored that Robyn Sandy, a dedicated and skilled change agent and a true visionary, has utilized The Change Cycle in her work to assist her country in becoming change resilient.

Our clients have made the past fifteen years of crisscrossing the planet in the name of change well worth every pretzel on every flight. We salute the efforts and successes of Amgen, Amcor, American Express, Avon, Beckman Coulter, Gateway, Gaylord Entertainment, Honeywell, Land O'Lakes, Lawson Software, Nestlé, Sensa Solutions, SONY, the U.S. intelligence agencies, the U.S. Department of Defense, and Wells Dairy.

Our heartfelt appreciation to our dedicated and loyal certified trainers who have successfully taken The Change Cycle into boardrooms, factories, top security installations, hospitals, and training rooms—everywhere. Some of the very best include Annette, Brad, Dan, Denise, Fran, Heather, Heidi, Jack, Jessica, Lee Ann, Linda, Lori, Margaret, Mark, Misti, Phyllis, Sharon, Shirley, Susan, Tom, Vicki, and Wynn.

Writing is hard. Editing is harder. Phillip Hanrahan is a gifted and skilled editor who gave these words syntax while keeping the message focused and real. He is the best and worth all the commas and metaphors on the planet. Thank, You, Phil.

With heartfelt gratitude to Mark Bryan—to have created this project with you was an opportunity and an experience of a lifetime!

What a pleasure to work with the diversely skilled and competent staff at Berrett-Koehler Publishers. Steve Piersanti is a great captain of a terrific team. Appreciation to the reviewers Deborah, Jackie, Jeff, and Peggy. Kudos to Susie and the talented people at PubServ!

A very special thanks to our family and friends who supported, encouraged, and fed us in many ways so we could finish this book on time: Andi, Andrea, Angela, Arly, Candy, Celia, Deb, Debra, Greg, Jack, Judy, Juley, Kay, Marcia, Mom, Nancy, Roger, Savannah, Susie, and Trish.

And a special acknowledgement of the twenty-four-year friendship that the two of us have enjoyed. The Change Cycle is both the culmination of all we've learned and a mere fraction of the journey we've shared.

About the Authors

Ann and Lillie are cocreators of The Change Cycle Series, built on their influential Change Cycle model, which depicts the six predictable and sequential stages of change. Their work is done through CCMC Inc., an international training and development company. Based in metro Washington, DC, and Durban, South Africa, CCMC is home to The Change Cycle Series training and product line.

Ann Salerno

A frequent guest of airports, Ann Salerno is an internationally known trainer and consultant who has guided people and their organizations through change in places as varied as New Delhi, Warsaw, London, Cape Town, and Ottawa, as well as in dozens of American cities. Following graduate work in public administration, she began her business career in management at General Mills, gaining recognition early on for her managing and leadership skills. Named a Master Speaker and Trainer by Citizens Against Crime, she went on to build her successful career in corporate training and organizational change, working with organizations and Fortune 500 companies ranging from the U.S. State Department, the Central Intelligence Agency, and the Canadian government to General Motors, Amgen, the GAP, the NCAA, and American

Express. Heralded for her ability to communicate successful change strategies in an entertaining, practical, and accessible way, Ann has attended the Josephson Institute's Organizational Ethics Program, is a member of the WinStar Foundation's development team, and serves on the board of directors for Operation of Hope.org. She has coauthored four books, including *The Divorce Solution: How to Go from Bitter to Better,* and, with Lillie Brock, *The Secret to Getting Through Life's Difficult Changes.* Ann makes her home in Louisville, Kentucky.

Lillie Brock

Born in L.A.—lower Alabama, that is—Lillie Brock took the country road to the city, studying psychology and education as an undergraduate and graduate student before devoting herself full time to corporate training, work that has brought her to cities all over America and throughout the world. A sought-after keynote speaker and gifted facilitator, Lillie has years of experience assisting organizations in the business and nonprofit sectors to develop and integrate productive change. Former national president of Citizens Against Crime, on behalf of which she taught personal protection to members of hundreds of organizations nationwide, Lillie is coauthor of *The Secret to Getting Through Life's Difficult Changes.* Her professional background also includes work as an educational therapist for emotionally disturbed children. Lillie's passion for helping others led to a significant life and professional change of her own: a decision to enter ministry full time. An elder in her denomination, she is currently pursuing a graduate divinity degree at the Episcopal Divinity School in Cambridge, Massachusetts. Lillie lives in Dallas, Texas, with her family.

www.ChangeCycle.com

About The Change Cycle Series

The Change Cycle™ Series product line is available via CCMC Inc., an international training and development company with offices in metro Washington, DC and Durban, South Africa.

We offer organizational training programs for general employees and all levels of management, with formats ranging from 60-minute overviews to two-day manager training sessions. Our training materials are available in Spanish, French, and English.

The Change Cycle Series is designed to assist people in gaining the perspective, tools, and vocabulary to accurately identify the specific issues and questions that are relevant to their implementation of organizational change. Via training, keynote presentations, and seminars, our certified trainers and facilitators provide pertinent skills to assist participants in taking personal responsibility for their reactions and responses within changing environments.

For more information about The Change Cycle Series

Training • Keynotes • Seminars

In the USA:
www.ChangeCycle.com
CCMC Inc.
800.878.8422

In South Africa:
www.ChangeCycle.co.za
Interchange International
031 – 764 4993

The secret of change is to focus all of your energy,
not on fighting the old, but on building the new.

Socrates

About Berrett-Koehler Publishers

Berrett-Koehler is an independent publisher dedicated to an ambitious mission: Creating a World That Works for All.

We believe that to truly create a better world, action is needed at all levels—individual, organizational, and societal. At the individual level, our publications help people align their lives with their values and with their aspirations for a better world. At the organizational level, our publications promote progressive leadership and management practices, socially responsible approaches to business, and humane and effective organizations. At the societal level, our publications advance social and economic justice, shared prosperity, sustainability, and new solutions to national and global issues.

A major theme of our publications is "Opening Up New Space." They challenge conventional thinking, introduce new ideas, and foster positive change. Their common quest is changing the underlying beliefs, mindsets, institutions, and structures that keep generating the same cycles of problems, no matter who our leaders are or what improvement programs we adopt.

We strive to practice what we preach—to operate our publishing company in line with the ideas in our books. At the core of our approach is *stewardship*, which we define as a deep sense of responsibility to administer the company for the benefit of all of our "stakeholder" groups: authors, customers, employees, investors, service providers, and the communities and environment around us.

We are grateful to the thousands of readers, authors, and other friends of the company who consider themselves to be part of the "BK Community." We hope that you, too, will join us in our mission.

Be Connected

Visit Our Website

Go to www.bkconnection.com to read exclusive previews and excerpts of new books, find detailed information on all Berrett-Koehler titles and authors, browse subject-area libraries of books, and get special discounts.

Subscribe to Our Free E-Newsletter

Be the first to hear about new publications, special discount offers, exclusive articles, news about bestsellers, and more! Get on the list for our free e-newsletter by going to www.bkconnection.com.

Get Quantity Discounts

Berrett-Koehler books are available at quantity discounts for orders of ten or more copies. Please call us toll-free at (800) 929-2929 or email us at bkp.orders@aidcvt.com.

Host a Reading Group

For tips on how to form and carry on a book reading group in your workplace or community, see our website at www.bkconnection.com.

Join the BK Community

Thousands of readers of our books have become part of the "BK Community" by participating in events featuring our authors, reviewing draft manuscripts of forthcoming books, spreading the word about their favorite books, and supporting our publishing program in other ways. If you would like to join the BK Community, please contact us at bkcommunity@bkpub.com.